ENDORSEMENTS

It is my pleasure to write an endorsement for Heather Z's beautiful and timely book, *Unlocking Heaven's Truth*. I have known Heather Z for several years, and I can confidently say this book carries her heart to the reader.

As she writes in Chapter 1, "My heart was filled with a deep sense of urgency and compassion.... Challenges and issues are part of life, but I believe God created you to overcome them all." In this book, you will learn of Heather's great difficulties and struggles, but you will also learn of her greater triumph through Christ—as well as how you can triumph over the tests and trials of life. Are you experiencing a life-threatening issue in your body? Are you suffering heart-wrenching emotional pain? Have you experienced a situation that has brought shame into your life? As I read these pages, I became so aware of the power of hope that will surround your own heart and mind, and establish you in a place of overwhelming peace as you read.

I love you, Heather. Thank you for sharing your story with us, your reading audience. You have shown us that no matter the challenges that come, God's irresistible love, His conquering power, and His loving arms are present to comfort us, deliver and restore us, and cradle us safely through it all.

Denise Renner
Minister, Broadcaster, Author
Moscow, Russia

In her book *Unlocking Heaven's Truth*, Heather Z shares her most intimate struggles with life and death, her hopes, her dreams, and how God was there with her during every trauma and trial. What we all need to remember, as she so beautifully describes, is that if you are willing to trust God, He is there for you. He is looking for every opportunity to show His power and passion for you. He desires to assist you in being made victorious and whole through Him. Discouragement can come when life dishes out many seemingly insurmountable trials, traumas, and pains. They can be emotional, spiritual, and/or physical. Heather takes your hand and shows you how she has been challenged beyond what seems possible to endure. But God can take the most impossible and ugly disasters and make them beautiful. Heather, thank you for your transparency, the glimpse into your life, and your love for walking with God. If He can do it for her, He most certainly can do it for you. You're not alone. Read Heather's story and let it encourage you to choose Heaven's Truth.

Teri L. Bailey
Author, Co-Host of Flash Point Army

This book will inspire, challenge and strengthen you. It moves you from fear to faith with an impartation of hope. I love how Heather emphasized that joy and laughter were as crucial for healing as medical attention. Heather encourages you to use your voice, speak out loud, stand in your authority and pray in the Holy Ghost and power. She'll show you how to dwell in the peace of God, which is your Goshen—the secret place of the Most High!

Annabelle Wallnau
Founder, Furnishing Families International

I recommend this book because it will equip, encourage, and provoke you to walk in the power of God's Word. You will learn to overcome the enemy by praying from a position of victory, not defeat. God will show up, and you will see and experience His end-time power.

Mechelle Murillo
Wife of Mario Murillo
Co-Leader of Mario Murillo Ministries

Some books inspire. Others challenge. A rare few have the power to shift something deep within you. *Unlocking Heaven's Truth* is one of those books. What makes this book stand out is not just the miraculous encounters, though they are breathtaking. It's the unwavering truth that God is still speaking, healing, and delivering today in ways that will shock you. Heather shares the raw details of her battles and invites you to step into the same supernatural life and victory she experienced. This book is a bold invitation to bring your trauma into the light, to fight for your healing, and to embrace the fullness of what Christ paid for on the Cross. So, open your heart and grab hold of this revelation because you might walk away with your miracle if you receive it.

Alan DiDio
Host, *Encounter Today*
Pastor, The Encounter Charlotte

Heather Z's *Unlocking Heaven's Truth* is an incredible, hard-to-put-down story of her journey of faith. I like that she is so open about the struggles and trauma she's faced, making it clear just how powerful God's presence is in her life. Through her raw and honest testimony, she shows how faith can bring healing and purpose, even in life's darkest moments. She doesn't shy away from the emotional toll of trauma or the unique challenges of ministry, making her story both relatable and deeply inspiring. More than just a book, this is a heartfelt message of hope, encouraging us to trust God and grow closer to Him. Heather's love for God and people shines through every page, making this a truly impactful read.

Leanna Brewer
Founder/CEO Spark Worldwide
Pastor, OpenDoor Church

From the first paragraph, I was completely gripped. Heather has bravely and transparently opened her life to unimaginable challenges, pain, and trauma. But what you will get through this book is the will to fight the good fight of faith despite all odds. You will be reminded of the faithfulness of our God to reach into our mess and create a miracle!

Jenny Donnelly
Founder, Her Voice Movement

Unlocking Heaven's Truth is a powerful and deeply moving testimony that will stir your faith and ignite hope in your heart. In this remarkable book, my dear friend Heather shares her extraordinary encounter between life and death, where God spoke to her in Heaven about her divine purpose and call.

Through riveting stories—like her miraculous healing from a spinal cord injury, a battle with a hereditary disease, the resurrection of her daughter, and God's intervention in her son's life—Heather boldly reveals that we serve a God who still performs miracles today. With biblical insight and personal experience, she unpacks how faith and action work together, empowering believers to exercise their God-given authority.

This book also powerfully reveals that through our faith in God, we have the ability to choose between life or death, blessings or curses—just as Scripture declares. If you've ever doubted the reality of miracles or found yourself in desperate need of one, this book will breathe fresh faith into your spirit. Heather and her husband Joseph are not only trusted friends, they are living examples of radical faith and love. This book carries an impartation that will awaken you to the supernatural possibilities available in Jesus' name.

Miriam Evans
Co-Founder of Revival Mandate International
Author of *Glory Miracles and Decrees That Activate the Gifts of the Holy Spirit*

Heather Z and her husband Joseph are some of the greatest people I know. They are powerful leaders in the body of Christ. In *Unlocking Heaven's Truth,* Heather shares her profound supernatural experiences and deep revelation of God's healing power. This book will lift your faith for the miraculous, grow your knowledge in the Word of God, and reveal Jesus to you. It is my honor to endorse this book.

Pastor Brian Gibson
Lead Pastor, HIS Church

I've had the privilege of watching Heather share these stories in person. I can't imagine a more powerful story than the one she has lived. This book will leave you amazed by the faithfulness of God. In every story and her daily walk, I see faith in action. Let it build your faith to stand in dark days.

Pastor Jessi Gibson
Author, Pastor, HIS Church

UNLOCKING HEAVEN'S TRUTH

Harrison House

Shippensburg, PA

UNLOCKING HEAVEN'S TRUTH

WHAT I EXPERIENCED BETWEEN LIFE AND DEATH

HEATHER Z

Published by Harrison House Publishers

Shippensburg, PA 17257

ISBN 13 TP: 978-1-6675-0971-6

ISBN 13 eBook: 978-1-6675-0972-3

For Worldwide Distribution, Printed in the U.S.A.

1 2 3 4 5 6 7 8 / 29 28 27 26 25

DEDICATION

I dedicate this book to you, the reader. I desire this to be a spark and a picture of hope that you need. Although our stories may not be the same, for those in the middle of a real-world life battle, I believe the Lord will speak to your heart and provide the encouragement you need.

The Lord is always speaking and ready to make the impossible now possible. This reminds me of Roger Bannister, the first to break the four-minute mile run. He was a picture of strength and an example, showing it could be done. His breaking a world record brought hope to other runners that they, too, could complete an extraordinary feat.

Even through impossible challenges, we can overcome and conquer with a full quality of life. There is victory on the other side of your battle. I'm here to tell you that *staying power* will help you see it through. Hold on and don't give up; you can overcome the darkest situation through *the blood of the Lamb and the word of your testimony* (Revelation 12:11).

My prayer is to shatter the illusion of isolation throughout those moments of dire straits in your circumstances—you are not alone. May the revelation of the Holy Spirit accompanying you and understanding how much Jesus loves you be the guiding force as you conquer the mountains along the path.

Allow the following verses to be revelatory and speak to your heart time and time again, enabling you to become fully persuaded and full of faith that will annihilate any challenge that has illegally harassed or tormented your heart. Jesus loves you, and there's nothing you can do to change that.

> *That the God of our Lord Jesus Christ, the Father of glory, may give to you the spirit of wisdom and revelation in the knowledge of Him, the eyes of your understanding being enlightened; that you may know what is the hope of His calling, what are the riches of the glory of His inheritance in the saints, and what is the exceeding greatness of His power toward us who believe, according to the working of His mighty power which He worked in Christ when He raised Him from the dead and seated Him at His right hand in the heavenly places, far above all principality and power and might and dominion, and every name that is named, not only in this age but also in that which is to come. And He put all things under His feet, and gave Him to be head over all things to the church, which is His body, the fullness of Him who fills all in all.*
>
> **—Ephesians 1:17-23 NKJV**

> *And now abide faith, hope, love, these three; but the greatest of these is love.*
>
> **—1 Corinthians 13:13 NKJV**

Above all, God longs to see you win more than you do. You will reclaim your life when your heart and mind align over this truth of faith. Start today, dear reader! Reclaim your life in Jesus' name. God is with you.

ACKNOWLEDGMENTS

Joseph Z, my very best friend and absolute love of my life. You are the one I have laughed with and cried with the most through this journey of victory. You have been an image of staying power, unbreaking through the hardest times. All your hard work and unwavering love for Jesus have been an inspiration. The picture of strength, hope, and love to continue in any situation has been the very support, aside from Jesus, that has helped me through life's trials. You were the one, many times, like a coach yelling encouragement to the fighter on the mat, encouraging me to keep going. Your voice in my head helped me to fight and even stay alive. You and the kids are the major reason I chose to stay and not give up or give in. I'm so grateful to do this life with you. I am blessed with the incredible life you have given the kids and me. We are so grateful for you and all that you do. Through your hard work, love for Jesus, and all you have done since you were young, we now receive the overflow from it because of your faithfulness, obedience, and never quitting or giving up. Words can't describe how thankful I am and how much I love you. Being your partner in ministry and in raising a family that is easy to love, and being your best friend is an honor. More than anything, it is an honor to be called *your girl*. I am enthusiastically excited for all the things ahead. The Lord has been so good, and I am blessed to share these moments in this life with you! I am your biggest fan and greatest cheerleader. I love you with all my heart.

Alison Joy, our firstborn. I did not truly understand what unconditional love was until you came along. You taught me the true meaning of love, aside from Jesus and your father, Joseph Z. You taught me something that I would have never known or experienced had you not come into our lives. Through this journey, you have been the spice of life, color, and downright laughter all along the way. I love you with all my heart and am thankful for you. Through this journey without you even trying, you have helped me laugh through it all. Love you, Baby Girl.

Danny Z, our second born. I was nervous as a young mom. While expecting you just after having your sister, thinking, *How can I love something more?* You taught me the *capacity of love*. You showed me how expansive love can be in a person's heart when you came along. The tent pegs of my heart expanded and were engulfed instantly from the moment I saw you to the present day. You have been the constant reminder that love is expansive and forever growing, and I am able to love not just as much—but more. I'm so grateful to Jesus that He gave your father and me the gift of you. Danny Z, I love you, son.

Jeremy Miller. I prayed for you like you were my own since the day I knew we were expecting a baby girl. I asked the Lord to bring a man of God, whether from another town, state, or even country. I see in you all the things I prayed for. I'm so thankful to the Lord that He brought us a son-in-law who is a true son. Thank you for being in our family. You truly are a gift from the Lord. I look forward to all the things that come through your life by the leading of the Holy Spirit. I love you, Jeremy.

Rick Renner, thank you for being a huge encouragement in writing this book. You are a constant reminder and an exemplary example of what is possible in running your race for the kingdom. Your prayers and input have meant the world to me. I am forever grateful and privileged to know you and have your voice in my life. Thank you, Sir.

Denise Renner, thank you for being my friend and influence in my life and ministry. I enjoy praying with you in person and over the phone. I am so grateful that the Lord brought you into my life. Love you, Denise.

Mary Ercoli, your dedication and amazing work ethic in seeing this project through to the final page are truly a gift. Thank you for your belief in this book. I am honored to work with you. I greatly enjoy laughing with you and calling you my friend.

Shanna Gregor, thank you for helping me create the clay in the workings of this book. You were a gift to help pull my thoughts into words in this project; and for that, I am genuinely grateful.

Arielle Carver, thank you for inspiring and exhorting me during my early thoughts about writing a book. You not only helped inspire me but also encouraged me through long conversations, vulnerable tears, and much laughter at the beginning of this process. Thank you for being such a great friend.

CONTENTS

FOREWORD

BY JOSEPH Z

Unlocking Heaven's Truth: What I Experienced Between Life and Death was an exceptionally powerful read for me. Empathy and a flood of memories came over me as I walked through each page, and being a firsthand witness, I recalled several of the stories Heather brought out. Her transparency and honesty powerfully moved me, ultimately finding myself at a place of reflection and deep gratitude to the Lord for His faithfulness.

Each valley and victory Heather relays reminds us of God Almighty's faithfulness and redemptive power. Heather's remarkable journey and unbreakable trust in the Lord brought tears to my eyes more than once while she brought to light defining moments of her history. For many, what Heather has experienced would be a life-breaking, life-ending tale. For her, by God's abundant grace, she discovered the rescuing power of our great God. She doesn't stop there. Heather is no victim. She is a warrior who has taken many things the enemy would have extinguished her voice with and turned them into a shout of victory.

Through her raw and emotionally forthright story, you will encounter the grief of tragedy and the delight of redemption. God, who causes all things to work for the good of those who fear Him and for those who humble themselves before Him as the Author and Finisher of their faith, will find inspiration through Heather's gripping story. Whatever has tried to steal, kill, and destroy you, you can overcome and know that it must be paid back in full!

From breaking her neck and visiting heaven to overcoming horrific abuse and contending for the lives of our children, Heather was and is a *champion* whom I have come to respect and adore more than any other person in this world. Her time of nearly dying constantly for five long years while living part-time in a dialysis chair was agonizing; however, watching her relentless stance of faith during that time challenged me to believe God for the impossible. Why? Because her faith worked! Heather is living proof that the promises of God, when held to, are irrevocable. Readers will find an example of someone who chose to believe in the name of Jesus and all His Word promises, regardless of what the circumstances look or feel like.

After years of talking with me about her journey to heaven, Heather felt it would benefit others if she shared it. I agree, as it has been a source of encouragement for so many who have been on death's door or have recently lost a loved one. Heather not only came through many trials and battles, but her journey ignited a passion within her to see people healed—spirit, soul, and body. A ministry of miracles has become a hallmark of her life—watching others live in the fullness God has for them.

In the wake of so many things Heather has gone through, powerful and legitimate results have come, which I have witnessed throughout her life. Breathtaking miracles, instant physical healings, emotional breakthroughs, and liberty from demonic oppression have been a constant throughout Heather's ministry as she ministers to others. To see her live out what she has proven by faith is a joy, and she challenges me constantly to live at a higher level of faith.

Tenured, proven faith that has outlasted death, sickness, abuse, and loss is something that terrorizes the kingdom of darkness, and Heather is a voice calling those things that are not, to come to life! Knowing Heather and watching her live out what she is preaching in this outstanding book leads me to say she is the best person I have ever known. Period. She is an exceptional wife and mother and certainly a dedicated co-laborer in the work God has given us to do. Full of integrity and honesty and walking in the Spirit of faith. I have never met anyone like her. Heather Z not only drives back darkness wherever she goes, she is also an agent of intense punishment against spiritual darkness!

It is my great honor to write a foreword and celebrate this tremendous book. I am thrilled to know that you, dear reader, can experience all the same victories Heather has and reclaim your life in the process!

To Heather Z, you are bigger than life in your faith and constantly challenge me to rise to what God has proposed for me. We stand today because of your belief in me and God's Word for our family. With all my heart, I bless you, love you, and celebrate all who will live to their highest level by laying hold of what you discovered and shared in the pages of this book. As we always say, "For Jesus." Because that is why this book was written—*for Jesus*.

With all my heart,

Joseph Z
Author, Broadcaster, Prophetic Voice,
and Husband to Heather Z

FOREWORD

BY RICK RENNER

An experience with death...suffering abuse as a young girl... and *receiving miracle after miracle in the face of longstanding impossibilities....* These are all part of the amazing story of Heather Z, who has faced more than her "fair share" of impossible situations that would cause many to simply give up. However, even on the very brink of death, Heather discovered the grace and power of God to deliver, heal, and restore her—and in this easy-to-read, riveting account, she shares her life-changing stories of supernatural intervention that, at times, were required for her to simply stay alive.

I read this book, *Unlocking Heaven's Truth: What I Experienced Between Life and Death,* from cover to cover. As I did, I kept thinking, I can hardly wait to offer this book to viewers of our TV program because it will be so enabling and empowering, especially for those who feel they are facing an impossible situation.

The truth is, there is not a person alive who hasn't experienced a deep hurt or some kind of devastating trauma. People may not disclose it, but *everyone* has faced something difficult along the way in life. However, in this book, Heather shows you that you do not have to bear such moments alone. She writes, in effect,

"A kept secret, hurt, or trauma has the power to destroy us, but when we bring it into the light, that's when healing begins."

In my own life, there have been times in years past when Satan tried to take me captive with lies that assaulted my mind. I write about this in several books, including my autobiography, *Unlikely*. I, too, learned that it's easier to fall victim to a lie when you're standing alone and not telling anyone what the enemy is trying to pound into your mind and emotions.

However, in her book, Heather shows that when a person dares to share that attack with the Lord and others who can help, it releases the power to decimate those lies, and the attacks are broken so that healing and wholeness can come. As Heather says, you'll find that regardless of what the enemy has attempted to do to you, it does not have the power to define you or set the trajectory for your future!

I've known Heather for a long time, but I learned more about her journey than I'd ever known as I read this book—including multiple dark moments she graciously shares with readers to bring hope to their lives. Heather makes it crystal clear that when any person finds himself or herself in a dark moment, it's easy to let fear take over, but that is when prayer becomes a vital lifeline to the One who hears every word, every cry, and every whisper of our heart. Heather states it so well: "Prayer has the power to lift us out of despair, silence fear, and align us with God's will, even when the circumstances haven't changed yet. When all hope seems lost, you can reach out and hold fast to Jesus, the only Hope we need."

I can honestly say that Heather is one of the strongest spiritual fighters I know, but even the strongest fighters get knocked down from time to time. And *whew*...the devil threw his best punches against Heather—she was the recipient of what should have been several *knock-out* punches! But instead of surrendering to them, she grabbed hold of the power of God to shake them off and declared, "No, this attack won't take me out. This fight's not over. I have more rounds in me, and I can still win!" In this book, she walks you through the process of how she indeed "shook them off" and will teach you step-by-step how you can do it too!

One challenge Heather faced in years past was a terrible sickness that took her to the edge of death and even beyond. She died in a hospital room and had an encounter with the Lord in which she discovered that her life assignment was not finished. He sent her back with the message that it doesn't matter how terrible the event is or what has happened to you, *God has a plan for your life!*

Due to my past episodes with attacks of the enemy, especially when I was a younger man, I was very drawn to what Heather writes about the sustaining power of God's presence. As I have personally discovered, Heather also learned about God's presence as a refuge during dark moments. She says, "When I felt the emotional weight of everything I was going through and faced doubt, fear, and frustration, I found peace in Him.... When life seems to unravel, God's presence is where we find everything we need. It's where we rest, recover, and regain strength. Like the Israelites in Goshen, we're reminded that God faithfully provides, protects, and guides us through every season. His presence is a promise, and that promise is unshakable."

As a recipient of a remarkable healing, Heather writes with confidence and authority: "Healing isn't always immediate, and miracles aren't always dramatic. Sometimes, it's just about hanging on—one more day, one more minute—until breakthrough comes. God is always faithful and present in those moments, carrying us through. He uses unexpected people, moments of laughter, friends who show up, and even those who can't. He teaches us to be patient with ourselves and others and reminds us that His grace is enough even when we feel exposed and vulnerable."

If you find yourself walking through a valley and feel that you're on the brink of giving up, this book will encourage you to hold on until the sustaining power of God brings you into the victory He desires for you. Heather writes that the journey isn't about a single moment of breakthrough, but about the mental and spiritual fortitude and perseverance to fight the good fight of faith and to keep engaging in it daily until you win.

From reading this book, you will discover that God will be faithful to you through it all. It doesn't matter how dark the night is; if you reach out to Him and allow others around you to help, you will find His light always shining and guiding you toward the wholeness you desire—and that He wants you to experience.

One of my favorite texts in this book reads, "The weakest among us is greater than all the forces of hell. The devil doesn't care that you're a son or daughter of God. He doesn't care that you have all the power and authority. His biggest fear is that one day, you might discover it."

As you read this book, I believe you will discover that the Greater One lives actively and powerfully inside you. And what He gives you, along with people around you to undergird you, will cause you to step out of the grip of hell's attacks so you can fulfill God's glorious plan for your life!

Rick Renner
Minister, Author, Broadcaster
Moscow, Russia

PREFACE

For years, I've carried a deeply personal story that I've kept close to my heart as I walked through life's ups and downs. It's the story of a near-death experience, meeting the Lord in a place between life and death, and the incredible journey that followed. I've shared bits and pieces of this experience, but I've never felt the release from God to fully share it in print with the whole world—until now.

Why am I sharing this story at this moment? The answer is simple: healing and wholeness. Over the years, God has taken me through a healing process in my body, mind, and emotions. I've realized that the story I've held so closely is not only for me; it's for you, too. I am a witness to the goodness of God: a truth-teller of God's faithfulness, power, and love. I believe God can use my obedience to tell my story and to bring hope, healing, and encouragement to anyone who reads it.

Many of us fight battles every day that we never expected. I know what it's like to feel overwhelmed, to wonder if things will ever get better, and to question why certain things happen. I also know what it's like to see God's hand at work, experience His immediate and miraculous power, and contend for healing over a long period. I've found peace while the storms of life raged all around me, and I've come out on the other side stronger and more grounded in my relationship with God.

I'm sharing my story now because I believe it's time to be transparent, to open up about the miracles I've witnessed, and to encourage you to keep going, no matter what obstacles tower above you. My story is about how God has held, shaped, and healed me on my journey to wholeness. I want to share my experiences in hopes that they will help you.

Sharing this story is an act of obedience, my way of giving back for all God has done in my life. I will do my best to articulate my experiences as best as possible. I pray that as you read my story, you'll find hope in your journey and see that God always gives you a way forward, no matter how dark things may seem. He has a plan for you, just as He had a plan for me, even when I couldn't see it.

1

BETWEEN LIFE AND DEATH

Raised in a faithful, dedicated Christian family, my journey with faith was deeply rooted in tradition and belief. Yet, nothing prepared me for the direct and transformative encounter with God I experienced at such a young age.

EVERYTHING WENT BLACK

At 14, I was a serious gymnast who practiced for hours daily. One afternoon, after a particularly intense session, my parents asked me to take a church friend's daughter to the park. My muscles were exhausted, but it seemed like a simple task, so we went.

I wasn't doing anything crazy—just swinging back and forth on a set of parallel bars, only two inches off the ground. But then, unexpectedly, my muscles gave out. I slingshot forward, hit my head, and heard a snap. Then—everything went black.

The next thing I knew, I was walking down the street, holding my neck. To this day, I don't know how I got up off the ground, but I believe the Lord Himself lifted me off the ground. I walked into our friend's house, and when my mom saw me, I said, "I think I broke my neck."

My body was so shocked that I could only manage a single tear. My parents rushed me to the hospital, and when we got there, the doctors told me they were going to take some pictures—a CT scan. Just a young teen, I had no idea what was going on.

As I lay on that cold metal table, waiting for the CT scan, I began to feel very tired. My eyes closed, and suddenly, I was looking down at my own body on the table. I experienced a calm detachment as I recognized myself from an outsider's perspective. It was such a strange experience, but I wasn't afraid.

It was just very matter-of-fact. I thought, *That's me on the table.* I left my body lying there. I felt an incredible peace. I didn't realize at the time that I was dying. It felt so real, yet I felt no fear.

The doctors examined the scan, and that's when they found it. I had broken my C1 vertebra, the bone that indirectly supports breathing by protecting the spinal cord, ensuring proper nerve operation, and maintaining structural alignment for airway and respiratory function. They call it the hangman's vertebra because, when it breaks, people usually die from suffocation when their lungs collapse.

I didn't realize at the time that I was dying.

AN UNEXPECTED TRIP

I found myself in an in-between place, where I could see people who were still alive and others who had passed away. It was almost like I was looking back at what was going on. I could see my mom. She and my dad were sitting together. The scene wasn't clear. It was more like viewing someone on a video screen during a meeting with a blurred background.

I wanted to invite my mom to come with me, but then I sensed a knowing in my spirit: *Oh, she can't come where I am.*

The people I saw were off to the side, within the in-between stage. As I was transitioning, I experienced a sense of earth and unity. The best way to describe it is as if I was walking by and I saw a group of people gathered, as if I were seeing people at church or in a circle talking. I could see their backs, and again, it was a form of light.

I had a sense of knowing that I knew them. It wasn't like I could say it was this person or another specifically. They were family members—my family. But to tell you a specific family member, I couldn't tell you that. They had an interesting translucency about them—like seeing a natural person on earth, but their appearance was exuded by light.

Everything was quiet, and I felt like everything was moving slowly. As I began to pivot away from my view of my parents, I stepped forward, and the colors started to change. Suddenly, I saw a house. I entered a place that felt very familiar—like my own home.

There was a big window, and I looked outside. I was so drawn to the vibrant colors in the grass and wheat.

The grass and wheat were completely alive—I was aware of them, and they were aware of me.

AT THE SPEED OF THOUGHT

As I looked outside, I saw the most beautiful grass I'd ever seen—vivid and full of life. Beyond the grass, I saw fields of wheat, a golden color I'd never seen before. I was drawn to it. As I began to walk forward, I thought, *I want to be out there.*

The minute I had that thought, I moved through the wall. My thoughts became actions faster than I could comprehend, and the transition from one place to another felt seamless.

Immediately, I was outside and found myself standing in the grass, looking at the wheat fields. It seemed as if I moved at the speed of thought. It was so simple yet mind-boggling.

As far as my eye could see was grass and rolling wheat. The grass was the greenest green, and the wheat a color of gold that I can't describe. It was almost like crystal. The grass and wheat seemed translucent and vibrant, alive in a way I had never seen. I was aware of it, and it was aware of me. I was completely connected to everything.

I just stood there in awe, completely overwhelmed. I can see now why the Lord says, "You cannot see My face" (Exodus 33:20). I found myself overwhelmed by grass and wheat.

His hands filled the sky, and it was a reminder of His infinite power and care.

I was taking it all in, as much as I could for a moment, and that's when I felt compelled in my spirit to look up. I lifted my eyes and saw two enormous hands filling the sky. I knew instantly—they were the hands of God, the Creator of the universe.

As His hands began to descend, I was overwhelmed by how they filled the sky.

Texas is known for its big sky, but the Texas sky looks tiny compared to all that this was. His hands filled the sky. As they came down and came together, if I was to blink, it happened within less than a blink.

THE ANSWER KEY

His hands came together, and suddenly, I was sitting in them. That's when He spoke to me. His words hit me in my abdomen, and I felt them resonate deep within me. It was a Spirit-to-spirit, heart-to-heart encounter.

When He said my name, I immediately tried to look up. In anticipation of His brilliance, I placed my hand above my forehead like I would to shield the sun's light from my eyes.

Again, it was indescribable, but I knew the brightness was there. I could look at the light, but it wasn't like I was *looking*. I was still trying to see, and I had no natural reactions.

Have you ever looked at the sun, and your eyes start to water, if it's bright outside? My eyes didn't begin to water, and I had no physical response. My eyes weren't filling up with tears. My body did not respond the same way as it would here on earth when looking at a bright light.

Rays of light were surrounding my hand as I shielded my eyes with my hand. I'm trying to look, but I can only see from His shoulder back down to where I'm sitting in His hands.

If you asked me if He was wearing a garment, I would say yes, but it seemed to be a garment of light.

I realized I could not see His face, so, like a little girl, I tucked my knees up to my chest, wrapped my arms around them, and sat there in His hands.

He began to speak to me, saying,

> "Heather, I created and designed you for a specific purpose. I have assignments for you on earth."

Even as a 14-year-old, I understood that God was speaking purpose into my life—reminding me that I was created for something greater than myself.

"I created and designed you for a specific purpose."

I began to sense a family and a husband in my future, tied to the purpose He was speaking about. His words filled me with a deep knowing of where I came from and who I was created to be.

He said,

> "I've designed you specifically for assignments. I need you for those; you're needed."

His words didn't carry much weight with me then because I was just 14. But later, after considering what He said, I thought, *Okay*.

As He spoke, specific assignments came to me in a rush, helping me understand what He was telling me. It would come *on* me. He'd talk, and it would hit me in the abdomen. I had a sense of family—my family, husband, children, and things I would do. I knew my assignment was what He created me for. I also knew I wanted to be good at it because that's what I was meant for.

People talk about their time in heaven, like, "Oh, I was in heaven for an hour." I can't say how long I was there. My conversation with Him didn't seem to last very long. But I have no idea. I had no sense of time. This conversation was very brief and to the point. I felt such a sense of purpose, love, and protection. There was no pain. The feeling of disappointment, hurt, whatever those things are, didn't exist there. I felt so protected. I knew everything was okay—even more than okay.

Then God concluded our conversation by reassuring me,

> "Heather, don't worry. Everything's going to be okay. I have you in My hands. It's time for you to go now."

It was a heart-to-Spirit conversation. It wasn't with our mouths.

I didn't want to go. I didn't want to leave. I told Him, "No, Lord, I don't want to go."

He gently repeated Himself.

> "Heather, don't worry, everything is going to be okay. I have you in My hands. It's time for you to go now."

It was a heart-to-Spirit conversation.

Just like that, my eyes opened, and I was back on the table in the hospital. I took a deep breath; air filled my lungs, and I started to breathe again. The doctors came back in, and they were stunned. They knew I should have been dead or at least paralyzed. By all medical knowledge, my lungs should have collapsed. But there I was, breathing on my own, fully alive.

The specialist who examined me was there by what could only be described as divine intervention. He had forgotten his pager at the hospital, which was unheard of for doctors to do back then. When he returned, they asked him about my case. He looked at my scan.

My mother said they told us, "Your daughter broke her neck, and you need to bring her back in six weeks so we can look at it again."

When we went back six weeks later, they took another x-ray and noticed something miraculous—the bone was completely healed, and all signs of my previously broken neck were completely gone!

The doctor said, "This is a miracle. We have to document this in the book of unexplained miracles." It was clear to everyone that something extraordinary had happened. They said I would not have survived if the break had been just a hair to the left or right.

The medical team put me in a soft collar to wear for six weeks, and after that, I was perfectly fine.

CREATED WITH PURPOSE

Even in dire circumstances, God is present and speaks purpose into our lives. God created each of us with a specific purpose in mind. He knew us before the foundation of the world (Ephesians 1:4-6). Before the earth was formed, God had a design and a destiny for you and me. He breathed life into us with that purpose in mind, and He's been speaking that purpose over us from the beginning.

I know this to be true because I've lived it. Remember what He said to me? He said, "Heather, you have assignments. I have designed you for a purpose." Those words have stayed with me ever since. God was present, speaking life and purpose into my heart, even in what should have been the end. I believe He does the same for each of us. No matter how dark the situation may seem, God is ready to remind us of His purpose for our lives.

The impact of the day I died, visited heaven, and came back continues to resonate in every part of my life. It became clear that my life was meant to testify to God's miraculous power and desire to heal and restore. I firmly believe God is intimately present and guides us. We all have unique purposes placed inside us by God Himself. No matter the circumstances, we are held securely in His hands.

I've also learned that just because God has a purpose for us doesn't mean it will automatically come to pass. We must partner with Him, obey His Word, and diligently guard our hearts. The enemy will try to use challenges, offenses, and all sorts of distractions to derail us from our purpose. But if we stay focused on God's Word and keep our hearts anchored in His truth, nothing can stop us from fulfilling the assignments He has given us.

God has a purpose for your life, no matter how dark your situation may seem.

What does this mean for you? It means that no matter what you're facing today—whether it's a personal struggle, a health crisis, or any other challenge—God is with you. He hasn't left you. He's right there amid it all, speaking purpose into your life. He's reminding you that He created you for something greater than the struggle you're facing. He's calling you to rise above the circumstances and walk in the purpose He's designed for you.

God is present in your life, even when things seem impossible. He is guiding you every step of the way. Your circumstances don't define you—God's purpose does. Guard your heart, stay close to Him, and watch as He leads you into the fullness of what He has planned for your life.

CREATED TO OVERCOME IT ALL

My heart was filled with a deep sense of urgency and compassion. I don't want you to miss out on something vital for your life—overcoming the challenges that come your way and living in the fullness of what God has for you. Challenges and issues are part of life, but God created you to *overcome them all.*

2

BRING YOUR TRAUMA TO THE LIGHT

You'd think that after such a miraculous experience, I would have been on fire for God, but life in this broken world has a way of pulling us down. Like the Israelites who saw the Red Sea part and still doubted God, I struggled even after experiencing a supernatural miracle.

Even though I'd experienced God's miraculous power, I had unresolved pain and trauma that festered in the shadows of my heart. I was a third-generation pastor's kid and saw the toll ministry took on my family. I didn't want any part of it. I was determined not to go into ministry because I knew how hard it could be. My parents were with other ministers all the time. This meant most Sundays were spent with ministers and church leaders. My parents selflessly spent countless hours in restaurants and green rooms (a place to wait until being called to minister), ministering and being present for ministry leaders, which was quite exhausting as a teenager.

By the time I was 17, 18, and 19, I had come to believe ministry was a waste of time. I remember sitting in a barbecue restaurant for four or five hours, watching my parents pour wisdom into a husband and wife in the ministry. I sat there listening to this couple make all their promises of what they would do from this day forward, and I'm thinking, *No, you're not going to change at all. You'll do exactly what you've been doing for the past fifteen years of your ministry.* My back was sore and hurting from sitting in that booth so long.

At that moment, I smoothed out a napkin, and with my pen, I started writing down what my life would look like in the future:

- I won't be in ministry.
- I'm going to live in Florida.
- My house will be on the beach with bright white and light tan colors throughout. Plants inside and out fill up the space.
- I am starting a job as a surgical tech. My salary pays all my bills, and I want to become a surgeon.
- I won't get married.
- I will never have kids.

I was deeply disappointed in this couple and ministers like them. At that moment, I realized I never wanted to pursue ministry because I had seen how exhausted my parents were from the countless hours they dedicated to helping others. I understood that 80 percent of these individuals were going to do only as much as they had to.

I witnessed compassion emerge in my mom and dad for these people. At the time, I didn't grasp that when God calls someone into ministry, it's a privilege, and He instills in them a heart to reach those whom others would reject. This is precisely how God used my parents to support countless individuals.

As a teenager, my understanding of ministry stemmed from observing my parents and other ministers. I saw how some ministers became consumed by ministry, pouring endless hours into others until they were drained. Because of this, I developed a skewed perspective on what ministry truly was. I didn't recognize that my parents and other ministers were working with all the light they had. I also failed to realize that God was using these ministers and my parents to fulfill their calling and reach those in need of a Savior.

During that period, I sought more from life. However, my frustrations with ministry seemed trivial compared to the trauma that would soon disrupt my life.

DEEP TRAUMA

When I was 19, I experienced something horrific that changed my life. A friend from the softball team invited me to hang out one night. He knew my parents were ministering out of town. I was a controlled, reserved person, aware of my surroundings, but that night something was different. We went to a pool hall, and I felt myself loosening up in a way that was completely out of character. I didn't realize it then, but my friend had slipped a mind-altering drug into my drink.

The next thing I knew, I was back at my parents' house, where my "friend" had brought me. I remember seeing another girl there and about three other guys. I don't remember how many men came through my house that night, but I know there were several.

It was modern-day trafficking—a night of multiple rapes, and I was so drugged that my memory was very hazy. It seemed like I was coming out of anesthesia after major surgery. I didn't remember how I got dressed or what exactly happened. The memories came back slowly, unfolding over time. I'm sure my so-called "friend" made a lot of money off of us that night.

The following day, I showed up at the house of the guy who had drugged me, and when he saw me, it freaked him out so much that he enlisted in the military and left town immediately.

I didn't tell anyone what had happened. I was ashamed, confused, and severely traumatized. I kept it all inside because I didn't want to hurt my parents. I knew it would devastate them. Out of my love for them, I stayed silent. I thought I was protecting them from the pain of what happened. However, this was not correct. I didn't understand then that my parents could have helped in ways that could have changed the course of my future.

Sadly, my silence sent me into a downward spiral, compelling me to make poor decisions and drift further away from God's plan for my life. It wasn't until I met Joseph, my future husband, that I began to open up.

HEALING FROM HIDDEN TRAUMA

Trauma, when kept secret, can lead to further pain and destruction, but sharing it can bring healing. It's easy to fall into a pattern of hiding what hurts us the most, thinking that if we bury them deep enough, they'll go away.

But the truth is...

They don't.

Instead, the hurts fester, creating a cycle of emotional pain that can be incredibly destructive. But I also know that sharing our trauma—bringing it into the light—can be the first step toward true healing.

Trauma, when kept secret, can lead to further pain and destruction, but sharing it can bring healing.

For a long time, I carried wounds that I didn't know how to deal with. We all have "go-to emotions"—those default responses we turn to when life becomes overwhelming. For me, these were fear and abandonment, patterns that felt familiar but kept me trapped. These emotions became like drugs, something I would reach for because they were familiar, even though they were harmful.

Fear and abandonment became my default reactions, emotions I turned to for years. As a child, the enemy planted seeds of fear and lies in my heart, and I believed and ran with them. The more I meditated on those lies that had no basis, the more they shaped how I responded to life's challenges.

Fear, worry, rejection, anger, and self-pity are all forms of meditation. When we dwell on them, we give them power in our lives. For example, I would be home alone for days. In these scenarios, I would use my imagination in what I thought was wisdom but was fear. I would create "what if" scenarios in my mind. "What if someone broke into my home? What if they attacked me?" My imagination took me down the path of creating a scene that eventually would end in my death. This is what I mean about the enemy providing the seed, but I allowed it to grow.

The truth is that fear is a liar. The acronym F.E.A.R.—False Evidence Appearing Real—perfectly describes it. The enemy doesn't need to keep working on us once we've believed his lies; we do the rest on our own. But we can break free from these patterns by turning to God's Word and meditating on His promises instead.

Looking back, I realize that keeping my trauma hidden only made things worse. It allowed those "go-to emotions" and "what-if" scenarios to take over, pulling me further into a cycle of pain and destruction. But when I finally chose to bring my pain to the surface, to share it and release it, I found healing that I didn't think was possible.

When we bring our trauma into the light, we open ourselves up to healing.

HEALING BEGAN IN THE HEART

God knew my feelings toward ministry and how I refused to participate. He knew the pain from the traumatic night at age

19. He also knew His plan for my life. The Lord has a way of healing hurts from the past. Remember the list I made at the table when I was young? It was written from pain and a false idea of ministry. God knew I needed healing of these mindsets to help me heal of my physical trauma. Throughout the following years, my heart began to change. The desires I thought were my own began to change into what I knew were the Lord's desires for my life. I didn't know at the time, but God had a person who would play a significant role in bringing healing from trauma and toward the life of ministry.

GOD'S PLAN UNFOLDING

My parents were conducting meetings in Duluth, Minnesota, and I was regularly partying in Minneapolis. One day, while I was making coffee at home, my dad said, "You should meet the youth pastor." This reminded me of my childhood prayer that my father would find my husband. My dad had never brought up a man or my future husband. I was his youngest daughter, and he was very protective of me.

The following weekend, I felt an urgency to attend the meeting my dad was discussing. I drove to Duluth and arrived during worship. People were sweating because they passionately and reverently worshiped the Lord. This was not an experience I was used to.

My parents were out to lunch the following day, and I couldn't find them. A random guy approached, asking if I needed anything. He knew who I was and invited me to lunch. He was the most non-threatening person I had met. He was different from the other guys. His name was Joseph.

PROPHECY AND PURPOSE

God's purpose for our lives was intricately woven into the prophecy Joseph received long before we met. This shows how God prepared both of us for the healing we would experience together.

When I met Joseph, I was terrified that he would reject me if he knew the truth. When our relationship started getting serious, I decided to tell him everything. I laid it all out because I didn't want to go into marriage with anything hidden. I was afraid he would reject me because I wasn't the perfect, proper church girl he might have been expecting.

God intricately weaves our lives together, even when we can't see the bigger picture. Our story is about prophecy and purpose. Long before we met, God prepared Joseph and me to navigate one of the darkest seasons of my life.

When Joseph was younger, he received a prophetic word from a globally recognized prophet in a prophetic meeting, a man known for his deep understanding of the prophetic. This prophet was working in the gift of prophecy by speaking a word of knowledge over Joseph. *Prophecy* is a spiritual gift God gives to communicate His truth, encouragement, or guidance through His people. A *word of knowledge* is specific insight or facts the Holy Spirit reveals about someone or something the person giving it could not have known naturally.

Joseph was beginning to step into his purpose. He had so many questions about his future:

- What was God's plan for him?
- Who would he marry?
- How would he serve the Kingdom?

Around that time, that prophetic word about Joseph's life would only make sense years later. The prophet told Joseph that God had chosen him to be a protector, that he would need to stand firm in faith and be a source of strength for the woman he would marry.

The man of God also shared something about me. At that very moment, as he spoke to Joseph, God was protecting and preparing the woman who would become Joseph's wife. He assured Joseph that God's hand was upon her, guarding her life and that she was being prepared for the purpose they would one day walk in together.

Joseph didn't fully understand what this meant then, but he held on to those words and tucked them away in his heart.

Fast-forward years, and when Joseph and I met, those prophetic words began to unfold in a way that only God could orchestrate.

When I told Joseph everything that took place in my past, I didn't know that God had been preparing us for this moment all along. When I told Joseph my story, he took time to process it. He didn't react immediately but sought the Lord in prayer. Those prophetic words the prophet had spoken over him came rushing back.

Joseph realized this was what the prophet had shared with him—that God had called him to be my protector, to stand by me through the healing process, and to help me walk out of the darkness that had overshadowed my life for so long. Joseph's response wasn't just an act of love but the fulfillment of God's prophetic word, showing how God had prepared him to stand with me in faith and healing.

Joseph's response became a turning point for me. He didn't reject me; instead, he stood by me and helped me walk through the healing process. His unwavering support showed me a picture of God's love and faithfulness.

Joseph also realized something even more powerful when the prophetic minister spoke those words. God was indeed protecting and preparing me, just as he had said. Joseph received these words the same year that I broke my neck. Even as I walked through the trauma and pain, God's hand was upon me, guarding my life and preparing me for the healing that was to come.

Joseph returned with a decision—not made out of obligation but out of love and obedience to God's call on his life. He chose to stay, marry me, and be the protector God had spoken about all those years ago. From that moment, our journey of healing began.

TRUST GOD'S TIMING

It wasn't an easy road, and healing didn't come overnight. Sometimes, it's a journey that requires us to keep pressing in, even when nothing changes. I've experienced this firsthand with my health challenges. When I was diagnosed with hereditary double renal failure, it took years of waiting, praying, and trusting God before I received a kidney transplant. (I will share that with you in a later chapter. The healing process was long and difficult, but God was with me every step of the way.)

There were days when the memories would resurface when the pain felt overwhelming. But through it all, Joseph was there, just as God had prepared him to be. He prayed with me, supported me, and reminded me of God's love and purpose for my life. I began to heal through faith, prayer, and my husband's support.

Looking back, I see God's hand in every part of our story. He spoke purpose into Joseph's life long before we met, knowing that one day, Joseph would need to be a source of strength and protection for me. It's a testament to God's faithfulness that He is present even in the most dire circumstances, speaking purpose and preparing the way for our healing and restoration.

SHARED TRAUMA INVITES HEALING

If you're carrying something today—if there's a trauma or hurt you've been keeping secret—I want to encourage you to bring it into the light. Don't carry it alone. Share it with God, with someone you trust, and allow yourself to start the healing process. Trauma, when kept secret, can destroy us from the inside out, but when we bring it into the light, healing begins. God's love and healing power can restore what has been broken, no matter how deeply wounded you've been.

It is important to find someone you trust to share your burdens with. Healing often begins with a confession—acknowledging that we're hurting and need help. When we carry our burdens alone, they only grow heavier. But when we share them, we invite healing into our lives. It's not always easy to open up, especially when the wounds are deep, but I know how transformative it can be.

I've also learned that it's easy to believe the lie that because something terrible happened to you, you're no longer worthy of the life God has planned for you. But that's not true. Healing is possible through Jesus, no matter how broken you feel. What happened to you doesn't define you—God's love and purpose for your life do.

For years, I struggled with feelings of inadequacy, believing that my past disqualified me from the future God had for me. But as I walked through my healing journey, I began to see that God's love is greater than any pain or trauma. His healing power is available to restore what has been broken. He wants to bring wholeness where there was once only brokenness. He does this for me and everyone who reaches out to Him.

The enemy tried to use my trauma to keep me silent and trapped in a cycle of pain and self-doubt. But God had a different plan. He used my willingness to share my pain and to open up about my struggles as the starting point for my healing. By bringing my trauma into the light, confessing, and sharing it with those I trusted, I began to see God's hand at work in my life in ways I never imagined.

I can't stress enough how important it is not to carry your burdens alone. Whether it's a trauma from your past, a current struggle, or an ongoing battle with emotional pain, sharing your pain with trusted individuals can be the key to your healing. God never intended for us to walk through life's difficulties alone. He places people in our lives—friends, family, counselors, spiritual mentors—who can help carry the load and speak truth into our lives when we struggle to see it for ourselves.

What happened to you doesn't define you—God's love and His purpose for your life do.

HIS WORD—YOUR PATH TO WHOLENESS

God cares about every part of you—your physical body, your mind, and your emotions. He wants you to be fully healed, whole, and restored. The blood of Jesus has provided everything you need, and He wants you to have all He's promised. Today, I encourage you to lay it before the Lord if you're struggling with emotional pain. Let go of the hurt, shame, fear, and anything else weighing you down. Speak life over your situation, and trust that God is working it all out for your good.

We engage in the healing process as we agree with God's Word. Sometimes God moves miraculously, bringing instantaneous freedom. No matter how long it takes, know that God is faithful and will complete the good work He has begun in you.

Let's pray together:

> *Father, in the name of Jesus, I thank You for the person reading this today. Lord, we receive Your healing Word. We declare that Your promises are true, and we stand in agreement with them. Right now, we speak forgiveness, release shame, and let go of anything that is not of You. We receive Your peace, healing, and wholeness in our hearts and minds. Lord, thank You for bringing the right people into our lives to assist in the healing process. We trust You and believe You are working all things together for our good. In Jesus' mighty name, amen.*

Whatever you're carrying, remember that healing starts with bringing your pain into the light. Share it with God and trust Him to begin the restoration process in your life.

3

BABY LIVE!

After Joseph and I were married, we had side jobs and stood alongside my parents in the ministry. We had worked through emotional and physical trauma from my younger years. As newlyweds, our marriage brought new challenges. A year after we were married, we found out I was pregnant. At around five or six months, the baby suddenly stopped moving in the womb—no kicking, no movement. She was motionless for three days. I asked my physician what was happening, and her words were clear and urgent: "Go to the hospital immediately and get checked."

That evening, Joseph and I sat in a busy emergency room, waiting for what felt like an eternity. Finally, they took me back for an ultrasound. The silence in the room grew louder as the technician moved the wand across my belly. No heartbeat. Nothing but quiet.

Joseph started talking to the ultrasound technician. Joseph's that way and always has been. Out of the blue, he'll ask people about what they do—the pros and cons of their job. He asked, "What's the most difficult part of your job?"

The technician said, "Honestly, a lot of times, the hardest part of my job is knowing that a baby's dead, and I can't say anything."

He was hinting—maybe trying to prepare us a little.

We were in our early 20s. We were ignorant of the process and naive to what he was saying. We responded, "Oh, wow. That's terrible. Okay." We were, in a sense, completely missing the fact that, *Hello, this could potentially be you.* We were young and naive, so we let the professionals lead us through the process.

However, when he said that about knowing the baby was dead, I did have a momentary thought. It wasn't until after the ultrasound, when we returned to the hospital examining room, that I immediately caught myself. *Wait, no, I'm not going to allow that thought into my mind that it could be a possibility.*

We went to the emergency room that evening after dinnertime. It was a hectic night in the ER, filled primarily with nurses, ultrasound technicians, and patients. We did a lot of waiting that night—waiting to become important enough for a doctor to enter our room. Other people arrived after being in major car accidents and all kinds of serious medical emergencies. I wasn't an urgent priority because of the lack of beds and room availability. It was a small hospital. We sat and waited a lot while they ran blood tests and other tests and rechecked them.

When they finally discharged me at 3 a.m., I was told, "Go home. Get a couple of hours of sleep. We will have your prenatal doctor call you in the morning to discuss your next steps."

BABY, LIVE!

By the time we got home, it was probably 3:30 a.m., and we sat on the couch. We needed a moment to come down from everything before we could even think about going to bed. That's when Joseph looked at me and said, "I just want to pray."

His prayer was very simple. He laid his hands on my stomach and said, "Baby, I speak life to you. Baby, live! Live in your being." He said it a couple of times. "I command this baby to live, to have life, and we bless You, Lord." It lasted probably 30 seconds. That was it.

When Joseph prayed, he wasn't uttering words of desperation but inviting the God of miracles into our situation. God's power was at work, even when we didn't see it yet. His simple, faith-filled prayer was a declaration of trust in God's ability to perform miracles in our lives, even when everything seemed unsure.

I don't know why I didn't ask Joseph, "Why would you use those words?" Instead, I agreed and said, "Yeah, live!" As I mentioned, I had a terrible thought and took authority over it. I grew up knowing it's necessary to take those thoughts captive and not speak them—words contrary to what God's Word says for my life (2 Corinthians 10:5).

Strangely, in the scenarios that were possible with the baby, the hospital didn't cover themselves to ensure they were not getting themselves in trouble. If they had started to talk to me about "the possibilities are your child is dead," I truly know the outcome would have been different. It would have been devastating. But I know now that the Lord protected me from the information.

When we find ourselves in the darkest moments, like the silence that filled the room during the ultrasound, it's easy to let fear take over. That's when prayer becomes our lifeline. Prayer is a direct line to God, who hears every word, every cry, and whisper of our hearts. James 5:16 (NIV) reminds us, "The prayer of a righteous person is powerful and effective." During these seemingly hopeless situations, our prayers carry our faith and trust in the One who can change everything.

Prayer has the power to lift us out of despair, silence fear, and align us with God's will, even when the circumstances haven't changed yet. When all hope seems lost, you can reach out and hold fast to Jesus, the only Hope we need.

It takes bold faith to trust that God can step into the most impossible situations and do what no human effort can. When Joseph laid his hands on my stomach and spoke life, we weren't trusting in any ability of our own to fix the situation but in God's power to intervene. Jesus says, "With man this is impossible, but with God all things are possible" (Matthew 19:26 NIV). That's the foundation of our faith—knowing that God can do far more than we could ever ask or imagine (Ephesians 3:20 NIV).

Prayer has the power to lift us out of despair, silence fear, and align us with God's will, even when the circumstances haven't changed yet.

Trusting in God's ability to perform miracles isn't about denying the situation and pretending everything is fine. Instead, standing firm in the belief that God is still able, even when everything points to the contrary. We didn't know what would happen after that prayer, but we trusted that God could do the impossible—and He did!

GOD BREATHED LIFE

We went to bed, and the following day, when I woke up, I felt fluttering. Suddenly, a foot raced across my stomach! She started kicking again. Looking back now, we know God breathed life back into a situation the medical team at the hospital had perceived to be hopeless.

In Ezekiel 37, God revives the valley of dry bones, showing that nothing is beyond His power to revive. (This powerful, faith-building story is worth reading.) Whether it's a dead situation, a broken relationship, or even a literal need for life, God is always attentive to His people's cries.

When we don't get an immediate answer, it can be easy to believe the enemy's lies that God isn't listening. But that's not the case. God hears every prayer, and His timing is perfect. Psalm 34:15 (NKJV) says, "The eyes of the Lord are on the righteous, and His ears are open to their cry."

In our case, God heard Joseph's simple prayer and responded by bringing our daughter back to life in the womb. "Behold, the Lord's hand is not so short that it cannot save; nor is His ear so dull that it cannot hear" (Isaiah 59:1 NASB1995). No situation is too far gone for God to reach into and restore.

God isn't looking for perfection in our prayers; He's looking for a heart that believes He can do the impossible. In 2 Kings 20:5, God heard Hezekiah's simple prayer and added years to his life. In our story, God heard Joseph's prayer and responded with a miracle. Don't underestimate the power of simple, faith-filled prayers—God moves through them.

"The baby is moving!"

Shortly after we woke up, the doctor called. I told her the baby was moving, and she said, "Wait, what?"

I told her, "She's moving, and she's okay."

Again, I experienced protection from information. Usually, a doctor would erupt with, "How's that possible?" However, the doctor stayed quiet because she was also a believer in Jesus. Perhaps she has a conviction about her words, too. I don't know.

We went to the doctor's office, and after she checked everything, she said, "This is miraculous. You're supposed to be having a procedure right now, but your baby's alive. You're fine. Everything's fine." She did caution me with, "If you start having any pains, bleeding, or spotting, call me immediately."

A week and a half later, we received a letter from the medical center where I had the ultrasound. The letter said, "We're so sorry for your loss. If you need grief counseling, please let us know. It's not your fault, and here is why this could have happened."

The words in the letter blew my mind. I had to read it twice. Then I asked Joseph, "Can you read this? Am I reading this right?"

We were moving to Minneapolis, and my doctor recommended that I see a high-risk delivery doctor. Again, I didn't think a thing of it. The Lord was protecting me from my thoughts. I thought, *Oh, this is great. I'm going to get the best care.*

There are moments in life, like the one I experienced, when the Lord shields us from certain things to help us bring forth what He needs on earth. He will protect you from certain circumstances or comments because He needs a specific outcome. He needed Alison to be here. I believe that 1,000 percent.

What we often see as the end is sometimes just the beginning of God's miraculous work. When we sat in the room with the ultrasound technician, everything pointed to the fact that our baby was gone. But that's when faith steps in, and prayer becomes the vehicle for God's power. Just as Jesus called Lazarus from the tomb in John 11:43, God can bring life into any situation that seems dead. God specializes in resurrection.

Alison was born healthy! She's married now; she's beautiful.

The same God who breathed life into dry bones and brought Lazarus out of the grave is the God we pray to today. As in our story, prayer is where the miraculous begins. It wasn't the ultrasound or the medical reports that had the final say—it was God's power, activated through prayer, that brought our daughter back to life.

Faith in God can turn what seems final into new beginnings.

MARKED FOR HIS PURPOSE

Knowing my life and the assignments the Lord has given me, I am certain Alison is supposed to be here for many reasons. Much of it has to do with the fact that she carries what Joseph has and what my father had prophetically. She has inherited gifts that function regularly throughout her life, and the Lord plans to use these gifts for His kingdom purposes. I believe the reason we weren't fully aware of what was happening in the ultrasound room was to protect us from the "what if" thoughts I struggled with in my younger years. Because of His protection, I never went there in my mind.

In our covenant, we have the gifts of salvation. There are seven things God gives through salvation (and we'll go deeper into that in a later chapter). But one of those seven gifts is protection.

God gave us free will, and we have free thought. We can govern it however we want. It's up to us. By protecting our thoughts and not becoming afraid or concerned, we allow Him to bring His will into and through our lives.

It was like the Lord said, "I need to put you in this bubble right now to protect you from their words."

People often think *I didn't do this or that, so I must have messed up my whole life, and God can't use me.* But God always accomplishes His will on earth. As long as your heart is toward Him and you desire to do His will, He will use you.

I think of baby Moses when his mother set him in the basket and enclosed him in a physical protection from the elements of the rapids and the river. Likewise, a level of encompassing needs to happen to get you from point A to point B. The Lord uses different forms of vehicles. For me, it was a mental vehicle. He was saying, "This is your destiny, and I need to see this fulfilled."

If I could imagine Alison as Moses, this was one of me setting her in a basket and sending her on the destiny He has for her. I needed this protection for this child because God needed to get her to a certain point in her destiny.

You are marked by God! Each one of us is marked. No one is an accident. Whether your parents were saved or unsaved, God thought of you first. He was your first, not your parents. He still has a purpose for everyone.

He designed everyone for a reason. He really did. If people knew that and understood their value on earth, they wouldn't look at themselves or treat themselves the same. They wouldn't talk in their mind and beat themselves up. They would genuinely have the revelation of—*I matter.*

You are marked by God!

We're not here just to breathe in and breathe out. Truly getting to know your Lord and Savior and having a deep revelation of Him will help you through anything that comes your way.

HEALING IS REVELATORY

My healing only came by revelation. The more I got to know God and spent time with Him, the more revelation I received.

How people understand God and their purpose must come by revelation. This is where you know—in the depths of yourself.

Once you know Him, you realize the Spirit who's inside you. You can't do it any other way. You have to place value in the carnal brain to get to know Him and His Spirit. Paul prayed, "That the God of our Lord Jesus Christ, the Father of glory, may give to you the spirit of wisdom and revelation in the knowledge of Him" (Ephesians 1:17 NKJV). You have to know Him to know you.

WHAT IS A MIRACLE?

My daughter's healing in the womb is a miracle. Let's talk about miracles for just a minute.

A *miracle* is simply impossible. Miracles occur only when God Himself defies the usual laws of nature or human ability. A miracle can't simply be explained with science or logic. God intervenes supernaturally in such a way that His power leaves us in awe.

Remember what the specialist in my case said when I survived the broken neck? He couldn't believe I was alive. He said, "We have to document this in the book of unexplained miracles."

Jesus walked on water (Matthew 14:22-33) and raised Lazarus from the dead (John 11:38-44); both were miracles because they were impossible in human terms. No one can walk on water or bring someone back to life after days in the grave. Lazarus' sister noted to Jesus that by that point, her brother's body would stink (John 11:39).

God operates beyond the limits of what we know and experience.

A miracle:

- Defies natural laws. God interrupts what we expect to happen based on how the world works. We've already established it can't be explained by science or reason—like water turning into wine or a storm stopping instantly at Jesus' command.
- Miracles have a divine purpose. They demonstrate God's love and power and often point people to Him. In the Bible, miracles frequently validated Jesus' authority or built faith in those who witnessed them.
- It is immediate or dramatic. While healing can take time, a miracle is often immediate and extraordinary. It happens in a moment and leaves no doubt that something supernatural just occurred. Think of the Red Sea parting or Jesus feeding thousands with just a few loaves and fish—it was instant and unmistakable.
- Brings glory to God. Pointing back to God, a miracle reminds us that He is present, active, and sovereign. Miracles often stir faith in those who experience or witness them. The purpose is to glorify God and often to help people understand His power and love more deeply.

Miracles are so much more than just an unlikely event or something extraordinary. It's that moment when God unmistakably steps into your world to show you He's not limited by anything you and I understand. He's at work to bring His plans for us into our reality.

God responds to simple, faith-filled prayers and can perform miracles. When Joseph prayed, his words were simple but filled with faith. Sometimes we think our prayers must be eloquent or lengthy for God to hear them. But God responds to faith, no matter how it's expressed. Matthew 17:20 says that even faith the size of a mustard seed can move mountains. It's not the length or complexity of our prayers that matters—it's the very Father we trust behind them.

God responds to faith, no matter how expressed.

I mentioned some of Jesus' miracles, but the Bible records many more from our miracle-performing Father. Let's look at a few that demonstrate His power over creation, nature, life, and death.

- God created everything from nothing, speaking the universe, the earth, and all life into existence (Genesis 1–2).
- God used Moses to part the Red Sea, allowing the Israelites to escape from Pharaoh's army on dry ground, then closing the waters over everyone who pursued them (Exodus 14:21-22).

- While in the wilderness, the Israelites were thirsty, and God provided water from a rock when Moses struck it (Exodus 17:5-6).
- God miraculously fed the Israelites with manna, a heavenly bread that fell from the sky daily, nourishing them in the wilderness (Exodus 16:14-15).
- During a battle, Joshua asked God to make the sun stand still, and God stopped the sun and moon, prolonging daylight so Israel could win the battle (Joshua 10:12-14).
- The king threw Shadrach, Meshach, and Abednego into a blazing furnace. They stood unharmed and miraculously walked out of the flames because God protected them (Daniel 3).
- In a showdown with the prophets of Baal, Elijah prayed, and God sent fire from heaven to consume the sacrifice, proving that He alone is God (1 Kings 18:36-38).
- Jesus was born to Mary, a virgin, through the miraculous conception by the Holy Spirit (Matthew 1:18-25, Luke 1:26-38).
- The ultimate miracle is that Jesus rose from the dead three days after His crucifixion, defeating death and offering salvation to all of us who will believe and receive Him (Matthew 28:1-10).

GOD CAN

God isn't bound by human expectations. In Isaiah 55:8-9 (NIV), God reminds us, "For my thoughts are not your thoughts, neither are your ways my ways." God's intervention often flips what we expect, reminding us that His ways are far higher and greater than ours.

What seemed like the end for us was the beginning of God's miracle. Our daughter's life shows God can overturn even the most dire situations. No matter how final things seem, God always has the last word. We may face moments when everything points to an outcome we fear, but we can trust that God's intervention can change everything, turning fear into faith and death into life. He is the God who does the impossible.

4

THERE'S ANOTHER WAY—JESUS!

When my children were young, Joseph traveled a lot. I was a tired mom with two frequently sick children. When our son was three, we visited the pediatrician's office to catch up on his childhood vaccinations. Nothing I'd ever experienced prepared me for what was coming.

Before that, he was walking and talking—a normal little boy. I have videos of him being a completely normal toddler before this. After they gave him shots in both legs and both arms, everything changed. We got home, and he was gone. He wouldn't respond or make eye contact and started flapping his hands. It was like he had disappeared.

By the time he was around three and a half or four, he still wasn't talking. Someone suggested we get him tested. We took him for testing, and they diagnosed him with severe autism. They said he would flap his hands for the rest of his life, never speak or be potty-trained, and likely sit and shake. After they gave us this awful report, I thought, *Not with my Jesus.* I refused to accept that. *We're going to get to work on this.*

I know every family and every case is different. There's no judgment here at all. If you're dealing with an autistic child, I want you to know you are anointed to do what you're doing. God's going to help you through it. We'll believe with you for your child to get better. I don't want anyone to feel like, "Wait, this hasn't happened for me!" I believe our story can give you hope. God can do anything.

I refused to let those words define my son's future. The doctors had their opinion, but I knew their diagnosis didn't align with God's promises in His Word. I chose to contend for his healing, even though I knew the journey ahead would be challenging. Faith and action would have to work together if I wanted to see change.

FAITH AND ACTION WORK TOGETHER

This was not going to be a miracle. It was more of a progressive healing that would take time, persistence, and trust. I continually spoke healing over our son, declaring God's promises even when I couldn't see any changes. I also laid my hands on him and prayed. For a long time, nothing seemed to happen, but I wasn't giving up. I knew God was working behind the scenes, even if the healing wasn't immediate.

We took practical, immediate action. We enrolled him in a specialized school program that provided intensive support for two years before kindergarten. We did everything we could do in the natural. It wasn't until he was five when we began to see improvement. Slowly but surely, things started to change. By the grace of God, my son began to speak, interact, and progress in ways that defied the initial diagnosis. Healing was happening step by step.

I've been asked, "How did you do that?" I had moments of frustration. I was just a couple of months into potty training and could feel myself becoming impatient with Daniel. I never showed it, not with him. It's just me; everybody's different. Having a child who has disabilities, especially on a social level, I cannot express the level of taxing it was.

Faith alone wasn't enough—I had to pair it with action and trust God for the process.

There are two kinds of caregivers:

1. The loving parent: Every person experiences it differently. Some deal with guilt: *How did I let this happen?* Some get angry, and then they get very short-tempered. This is usually when parents bring in the second kind of caregiver.
2. The professional: They are trained and there to help in development.

I didn't do that. I prayed every day, strongly believing that "Lord, You didn't do this." My first response was critical. While not everyone shares the same belief system, many people accept a diagnosis as permanent when they first hear it. I'm not of that mindset. I responded, "No, absolutely not." I would remind myself that *there's another way. I've just got to find my other way—what works for Daniel.*

I experienced moments of exhaustion and tiredness. I would think, *Why isn't this working?* I quickly learned that spending every day with the Lord was vital. However, I always felt I had to develop a new game plan.

We were in ministry 24 hours a day, around other people, and attending conferences, so I always felt like I was constantly trying to devise a new game plan. Desperate, I whispered, "Lord, You have to help me. I don't believe them. I know he can be potty-trained."

With autism, certain trigger words or key phrases can help unlock understanding, allowing children to connect with your words and respond appropriately. I truly asked for wisdom. "Holy Spirit, how can my son hear it? What is the sound that he needs to hear so he understands to have the results of what needs to happen here?" It was a reward system for him every day. I pulled on the Holy Spirit, knowing my son's situation was unlike anyone else's.

Your first response is always the most important—it sets the tone for the battle ahead.

For my son, this wasn't the life God intended for him, so I pressed into prayer. God revealed the key that unlocked his mind and heart for answers to whatever he was dealing with. I think that's what parents with children on the spectrum or with any other condition have to do. They have to go to the throne of heaven for their child and say, "God, show me what it is"—because the child can't do it.

Your first response is always the most important. It's your first response to that assault. It's like street fighting. You can get sucker punched, and it can take you off guard, but you have a second to determine how you're going to respond.

In the case of a fighter, if it's their first time getting knocked down, they go through a mental process. They panic. They don't know what to do with that. As for other fighters who have been through it and are already familiar with a form of defeat, they have a better mental fortitude. They can shake it off quickly and decide, *No, that won't take me out. Let's go. This fight's not over. I have a few more rounds in me, and I can still win.* And that's you!

That's how it was with Danny. It was my first response. I didn't take that first diagnosis as defeat. I declared, *No, I've got Jesus. That doesn't apply to my family. There's another way.*

You can do that, no matter what it is—sickness, financial bankruptcy, a failed business endeavor that you put your all into, you dumped your heart and soul into making something, an art project you want to make live, and it's not successful, it fails financially. Some people take that as defeat, hang it up, and return to a nine-to-five job. If you can look beyond that and say, "No, there's another way," you ignite hope.

That's what I did with Danny. That's what I do with everything. There is another way—and His name is Jesus.

FACING THE ENEMY'S LIES

The enemy does not want our kids to succeed. He's trying to steal from us in every way possible. Throughout this process, I knew the enemy wanted to steal from my son and our family. There were moments when fear crept in, especially when we faced new challenges.

When my son was in second grade, we faced another challenge: he began having recurring nightmares. It felt like another attack on his progress, but I was determined to protect him—spiritually and emotionally. While I was having a sensitive moment, the Holy Spirit asked me to ask Daniel, "What's your favorite class in school?"

Daniel replied, "Meditation."

With that answer, I said, "EXCUSE ME?!" He was at a public school. His favorite class should be gym, or art, or something. I said, "What class is that?" (The Mama Bear was coming out.)

He said, "It's when we have our pads, and we lay down, and if somebody's angry, we talk about the angry octopus and how the sea child comes to us to help calm us down."

I flew into action. I immediately grabbed the phone and insisted on a parent-teacher conference! I wanted to know what was going on at that school. After meeting with the teachers, I discovered they were using New Age practices. The poses and breathing curriculum were created by a psychic. After they explained the process, I told them, "I would like to volunteer and teach the kids to pray to Jesus and to learn about the gifts of the Holy Spirit with the evidence of speaking in tongues." That didn't go over well with the public school system.

Needless to say, I ended up removing Daniel from this school. I had to set clear boundaries for what happened when I wasn't with him. This was part of my fight—not just for my son's healing but for his spiritual well-being. There were so many moments when I had to stay vigilant and stand firm in my faith, trusting that healing and wholeness were meant for my son.

PROGRESS AND SMALL VICTORIES

One of the most important lessons I've learned through this journey is the value of celebrating small victories. No matter how small, every bit of progress was a sign that God was working. We went from 12 specialists to none. We celebrated every new word, every moment of eye contact, and every step toward normalcy.

It was a long, step-by-step process, but I never let go of the truth that Jesus was with us every step of the way. Even in the darkest moments, God was present, guiding me through. His Word became my lifeline, reminding me that healing belongs to us as believers.

MIRACLES AND HEALING

In the previous chapter, we discussed how miracles are extraordinary, supernatural interventions in which God disrupts the natural order of things to display His power and glory. They are sudden, often unexplainable events that defy human logic or scientific explanation. Again, they are signs that point directly to God's faithfulness and are often used to reveal His purposes or confirm His messengers (like Jesus' ministry in the Gospels).

A miracle undeniably demonstrates God's hand in a situation, often occurring instantly and unexplainably.

On the other hand, healing is a form of God's intervention that restores health, wholeness, or well-being. It can occur supernaturally or through natural means. Healing may involve a gradual process in which someone recovers from sickness or emotional wounds over time, or it may happen instantaneously, as in the many physical healings Jesus performed.

I mentioned a few in the previous chapter, but let's look at a few more:

- Jesus healed a man born blind, restoring his sight and faith (John 9:1-7).
- Jesus raised Jairus' daughter from the dead, showing His power over death and His compassion for a grieving family (Mark 5:21-43).
- He healed a woman with an issue of blood who had suffered for 12 years (Luke 8:43-48).
- He healed a paralyzed man, forgiving his sins and restoring his walking ability (Mark 2:1-12).
- When Peter cut off the ear of a man during Jesus' betrayal and arrest, He restored the man's ear before being taken away (Luke 22:50-51).

Each miracle points to Jesus' love for us and His power to transform lives physically and spiritually. He is the same yesterday, today, and forever, and still able to perform miracles in our lives (Hebrews 13:8).

What the doctors said was impossible, God made possible.

While all healing ultimately comes from God, it may work through medical treatments, emotional restoration, or supernatural power. Healing reflects God's compassion and care for our bodies, minds, and souls, often showing His desire for us to be whole in every aspect of our lives.

The key difference is that while both are divine works, miracles are immediate and direct and often defy natural laws. Both reveal His presence, power, and love for His people.

But whether your healing comes instantly or over time, the key is to engage your words and faith. Begin by acknowledging your situation and speaking to God about it.

A great example of this occurred in Jesus' ministry when a father brought his son to Jesus for healing (Mark 9:14-29 NIV). Jesus tells the man, "Everything is possible for one who believes." Immediately the father says to Jesus, "Lord, I believe; help my unbelief!" (Mark 9:24 NKJV). This father's words capture the tension many of us feel between faith and doubt. He acknowledges his belief in Jesus but admits the weakness of his faith, asking for help to overcome it.

Sometimes, I would stand on the Word and apply my faith to Danny's situation, but the "whys" would try to flood my brain. In a sense, I was functioning in what this father did. "I believe, but, God, if there is unbelief in me, help!" The way to overcome these thoughts is to remain in the Word. Devour it, speak it, and it will start to remove all obstacles to where you can fully say, "I believe!"

This is a form of washing your mind with the water of the Word. Joshua 1:8 (NIV) states, "Keep this Book of the Law always on your lips; meditate on it day and night, so that you may be careful to do everything written in it. Then you will be prosperous and successful." This verse is the formula that we need to use daily. Having the Word in our mouths, meditating on it daily until we believe what it says, and then it will come out of us in our actions. Through this process, we can overcome all unbelief and see victory in areas that seemed impossible.

I'm excited to say that Daniel is a young adult who is thriving and working in media, creating 3D animations. He's a creative and talented young man who now contributes to our ministry, using his gifts to glorify God. This is a testimony to God's faithfulness and the power of prayer. What the doctors said was impossible; God made possible.

Looking back, I realize God was always with me, even in the darkest moments. We live in a broken, fallen world, and terrible things happen, but Jesus is with us through it all. His Word has principles that we must learn and apply, but more than anything, it's about discovering who Jesus is and understanding His deep love for us. That revelation brings true healing—so complete that it's as if nothing ever happened.

We know that healing isn't always instantaneous. Sometimes, it's a process in which you must hang on to what the Word of God says and what the Lord has provided for you. Sickness is illegal against your body if you're a believer in Jesus. You must hang on and know what you have until you become so fully persuaded that what belongs to you is yours.

God is faithful, and His healing power is available to everyone. Whether you're dealing with physical illness, emotional pain, or spiritual wounds, Jesus has already provided healing. It's up to us to receive it by faith.

5

GETTING OUT OF THE CHAIR OF DOUBT

I know today you might be facing your battles as you read these words. I know what it feels like to hear the worst possible news, to face impossible odds, and to feel like you're losing everything. But I also know God is with us in those darkest valleys. He never left me, and He will never leave you.

We've established that healing doesn't always happen instantly. Sometimes, it's a journey that takes us through the deepest valleys and over the highest mountains. The journey can also involve doubt, fear, and setbacks. Through it all, we discover that God's love is constant. His presence is our refuge, and His promises are true, no matter our circumstances.

I needed His presence even more as I began another battle for my life.

Everything started so suddenly. I was in the middle of leading a ministry meeting when I felt a sharp pain strike my stomach. I managed to get through the whole meeting, but by the time I returned home, the pain had intensified. It was so excruciating that it doubled me over—I couldn't move.

I called Joseph. He had planned to stay at the meeting until much later that night. I told him, "I don't know what's wrong, but something's not right. Please come home." Thankfully, he came immediately and brought friends to stay with the kids while we headed to the emergency room.

The doctors couldn't understand how I was still alive.

The doctors discovered cysts had ruptured, causing intense pain, but that wasn't the worst of it. When they tested my blood and checked my vitals, they learned that my kidney function was severely impaired. My creatinine levels—indicating the toxin buildup in my body—were dangerously high.

Essentially, my kidneys weren't processing the toxins, and the doctors couldn't understand how I was still alive. They told my family it might be time to say goodbye, unsure if I'd make it through the next few days.

I remember the moment the doctor delivered that grim news. Joseph and my mom were in the room. I don't even think we spoke after the doctor left. It was that kind of silence you often experience when no one knows what to say. The silence hung heavy in the air until Joseph broke it—not with despair but with determination. Joseph got angry. I mean, he got MAD. He wasn't about to let the doctor's words be the final say. He prayed over me with intensity, rebuking every word of death the doctor had spoken and declared, "You will live in Jesus' name!" He refused to allow space for fear or despair to take hold of me or our situation.

I knew from all that I'd learned battling for health and healing that my first response to this news would set the tone for everything that would follow, so I kept quiet, and all three of us just prayed.

THE BEGINNING OF DIALYSIS

Following the doctor's instructions and referral, I began seeing a nephrologist and a kidney specialist. My condition remained critical. During one appointment, I ate food I didn't realize would worsen things. It was loaded with tomatoes, which are highly acidic and put additional stress on my kidneys. That night, the pain returned, and the next day, the nephrologist told me I needed a port placed for dialysis.

They inserted a port—a tube that tunneled from my skin down to my heart—allowing the dialysis machine to filter my blood. Typically, ports like these are used for about three to six weeks, but nothing about my situation was typical. I ended up with my first port for six months.

The port brought countless challenges. The pain made simple tasks like getting dressed or washing my hair incredibly difficult. I still remember standing in front of the mirror, tears streaming down my face because lifting my arm to curl my hair hurt so much. But I kept pushing myself. I continued attending ministry meetings, dressing up, and trying to look put together because that was what everyone expected of me. It was exhausting—physically, emotionally, and spiritually.

I needed multiple ports—three in total. Each port required surgery for the port to be inserted in separate locations on my body at certain time intervals throughout the dialysis process. Every surgery brought a different set of complications.

One of the worst experiences was waking up during one of the surgeries. I remember the feeling of being awake but unable to move or speak, and I could hear the doctors working. Terrified, I kept thinking, *Why are you stabbing me in the neck?* Because my body doesn't take to drugs so well, I was able to speak and ask them, "Why are you stabbing me in my neck?" I could feel the sharp pain in my neck from what was happening. I felt everyone freeze as they proceeded to start again. I said it once more, and they all stopped for a second time and said, "We're going to get you some more meds."

I heard the hiss of the machines and felt my eyes flutter, and I was out. Joseph waited in the waiting room for a total of two and a half hours, which was three times longer than expected. He was very concerned at this point. As soon as I heard his voice, I started to cry because I knew I would be okay and was aware that I was out of surgery. The memory of that experience still lingers.

I needed to hold on to God's promises, no matter what my circumstances looked like.

The removal process was traumatic. I remember feeling them yank the tube, the pain shooting through my chest, and my body involuntarily rising off the table. I was streaming tears and said, "Ow," very softly. I know I was crying because the nurse was patting my eyes with a tissue. I could feel the tears running. The doctor was kind and asked everyone to stop. He talked me through, describing what he was going to do next by administering more anesthesia. It was one of the most challenging things I'd ever experienced. But through it all, Joseph was right there, ensuring I was cared for and protected.

Through it all, Joseph stood by me, advocating for me. Another time, when the medical staff wanted to remove one of my ports by simply yanking it out, Joseph refused to let them do it that way. He insisted on sedation, and I'm so thankful he was there. They tried to brush him off, saying, "We do this all the time; it's no big deal," but Joseph wouldn't have it. He demanded they take proper care of me, and thankfully they listened. I had already been through so much trauma—I didn't need any more unnecessary pain.

WALKING OUT OF DIALYSIS

During this time, Joseph and I started listening to Andrew Wommack's teachings on healing and faith. His words about the finished works of Jesus and receiving healing by faith resonated deeply. Through the finished works of Jesus, healing is something already done, something we can receive by faith. Hope that laid dormant in me began to stir. I started to believe I could be healed. While sitting in the dialysis chair, I listened to Scripture and teachings that built up my faith. I knew I needed to hold on to God's promises, regardless of my circumstances.

One day, as I sat in that dialysis chair, I heard the Holy Spirit say, "You're healed. Get up and leave." I didn't hesitate. I waved down the nurse and told her I was leaving. She tried to convince me to complete the session, but I knew what I had heard. God had spoken to me. So, I got up and left.

In the days that followed, I started feeling better—really better. My body wasn't retaining water, and my energy was returning. It felt like a miracle! I was excited to share the good news with those closest to me.

But their reaction wasn't what I expected.

One person told Joseph, "If she dies, it's your fault."

Their words cut deep. Doubt took root.

Was I really healed?

Could I trust what I had heard from God?

Slowly, those seeds of doubt grew, and soon, I felt unwell again. Eventually, I found myself back in that dialysis chair.

THE EMOTIONAL TOLL

Returning to dialysis felt like a huge failure. I was overwhelmed with shame and regret. I kept thinking, *How could I have lost my healing? How could I let myself get back here?* The emotional toll was immense.

I remember sitting there, tears streaming down my face, pounding my fists, and crying out, "God, what do You want from me? How do I get this back?" Everything I believed for and fought for seemed to have slipped through my fingers.

God wanted all of me!

God spoke to me again in that moment of complete desperation: "Get to know Me. Fall in love with Me for real, to the point that you don't care if you live or die."

It wasn't about the healing anymore—it was about Him. God wanted me—all of me, without conditions, without the need for proof of His power. He wanted me to trust Him, to fall in love with Him entirely, whether I was healed or not.

MY LAND OF GOSHEN

From that point on, I decided to seek God like never before. I made it my mission to know Him. I spent time with Him daily, not because I felt obligated, but because I deeply desired to know Him. Whether in the dialysis chair, caring for my children, or trying to get through the day, I reached for God's presence. I found comfort and peace in His presence.

I began to understand that His presence was my Goshen—my place of safety, my refuge in the storm. It didn't matter if I was still sick or struggling; what mattered was that I was with Him, and He was with me.

To help explain what I mean when I say, "His presence was my Goshen," I have included a section from Joseph's book *Breaking Hell's Economy*:

> **Light in Their Dwellings**
>
> Although the world is willingly and rapidly plunging into modern darkness, there is great hope and answers. The real church of the Lord Jesus Christ will rise to meet this oncoming darkness!
>
> Egypt is a representation of the world and its system. When darkness struck the land and its ungodly culture, Egypt became completely crippled, locked down, and in a state of utter dread.
>
> In Goshen, the experience was very different. The people of God did not experience the same things the Egyptians did. They likely could see the darkness—it is also possible they could sense the heaviness and terror of the Egyptians—but they had God on their side. There was no darkness within the houses of Goshen.
>
> At the very end of verse 23 in Exodus 10, we see something thrilling! "But all the children of Israel had light in their dwellings." This was no ordinary light! This Light the people of God possessed was supernatural! It shone in the darkness, in each of the dwellings of the righteous! Reminiscent of the Book of Revelation 21:23, "The city had no need of the sun or of the moon to shine in it, for the glory of God illuminated it. The Lamb is its light." It is this

light of God that is present within God's people that dispels all demonic darkness.

As this world plummets further into a darkness scenario, we must embrace the revelation of "the Light in Goshen." This Light was in their personal dwelling. This light is Jesus. To them, God willed to make known what are the riches of the glory of this mystery among the Gentiles: which is Christ in you, the hope of glory. —Colossians 1:27

—Joseph Z,
Breaking Hell's Economy, pp. 32-33

God's presence became my refuge during the darkest moments.

God's presence does all that for us today but in an even deeper way. I say that God's presence is my Goshen because of Jesus. Through Him, we have access to the Father (Hebrews 10:19-22). Jesus is our Provision (the Bread of Life), our Protection (our Good Shepherd), and the One who sets us apart (making us a holy people). His Spirit living within us means we don't have to travel to a physical location to experience Goshen—we carry it wherever we go.

God's presence became everything to me. It was my refuge during the darkest moments. When I felt the emotional weight of everything I was going through and faced doubt, fear, and frustration, I found peace in Him. It was no longer about getting out of dialysis or receiving physical healing—it was about my relationship with God. He showed me that His love, peace, and presence were more than enough.

When life seems to unravel, God's presence is where we find everything we need. It's where we rest, recover, and regain strength. Like the Israelites in Goshen, we're reminded that God faithfully provides, protects, and guides us through every season. His presence is a promise, and that promise is unshakable.

TRUSTING GOD'S PRESENCE IN THE VALLEYS

I can tell you that the valleys were some of the hardest times I've ever experienced. I faced surgeries, complications, and moments of waking up in the middle of procedures, feeling completely vulnerable. The doctors and nurses didn't always understand what I was going through. They saw me as just another patient, but Joseph and I knew I was not alone. God was with me in every operating room, every dialysis session, and every moment I felt afraid.

I spoke over my situation daily, declaring this was not the end of my story.

There were days when it felt like I was fighting a losing battle. The multiple ports, the painful removal process, and the shift to using my veins for dialysis were all significant struggles. I remember the fear I felt when they moved me to use my veins because it felt so permanent. The dialysis machine needed large needles to cycle my blood, and my veins had to be stretched to accommodate them.

The process was incredibly painful, and it took six weeks even to get my veins ready for the first use. Once they were ready, I had to start slowly, building up to a point where the doctors felt confident that this was sustainable. It felt like such a discouragement as if I was losing hope of ever being free from dialysis.

But even then, I remember praying, "God, this is not permanent. I know that You have more for me." I spoke over my situation daily, declaring this was not the end of my story. I would look at the dialysis equipment and say, "You're temporary, too." Speaking God's Word over my life became a way of life. I wasn't just fighting for physical healing; I was fighting for my faith, hope, and relationship with God.

Even though I was still in treatment, I knew He had not abandoned me.

SMALL VICTORIES

I remember the first time I got to take a real shower again after using the vein dialysis. For two years, while I had the ports, I couldn't shower. I could only take baths and had to wrap everything in plastic to keep it from getting wet. I'll never forget that first shower—just feeling the water running over my head. It was such a simple thing, but it brought me to tears. I cried because it reminded me that God was still with me, even in the small victories. Even though I was still in treatment, I knew He had not abandoned me.

HOLD ON TO HOPE

I share my story now because I know many people are walking through their valleys. You might face health challenges, loss, or situations that feel impossible. I want you to know that God is with you in the darkest valleys when you feel you can't go on. He is with you in the dialysis chair, in the hospital room, in the silence of your doubts and fears.

Healing doesn't always come how we expect it or when we want it to. But I've learned that God is always there, and His presence is enough. He wants us to seek Him, know Him, and find peace in Him. Physical healing is wonderful, but the real healing comes when we find ourselves in Him—when we realize that His love is enough, His presence is our refuge, and His promises are true.

No matter what you face today, I want you to know that God's love is enough to carry you through. He is your *Goshen,* your place of safety, and He will never leave or forsake you. Keep seeking and trusting Him, and let His presence be the refuge you need.

6

SHOULD I STAY? OR COULD I GO?

I want to share my journey, not just through the physical battle of dialysis but also through the spiritual and emotional battles I faced along the way. There were moments I could have given up—moments when it seemed easier to let go than to keep fighting. But God had something else for me, and I chose to stay. I faced choices that, for most, were small, like navigating a TSA checkpoint, but then they were as crucial as deciding whether to keep fighting for my life.

I once got in trouble with the TSA at the Denver Airport during a Global Entry appointment with a US Customs and Border Protection officer. Global Entry provides expedited US customs screening for international air travelers entering the United States.

The TSA personnel took me back to a private room. It's not like at the kiosk like they do now. I was doing everything she asked—scanning my eyes, answering questions—until we got to the part where they needed my fingerprints. When I put my fingers on the pad, nothing. We tried five different variations of things.

Finally, she started asking me strange questions:

"Do you work with heavy solutions like cleaners; do you clean houses? Do you clean your house?"

And I'm thinking, Yes, like a normal person. I clean my house.

She's looking at me sideways and says, "Do you do this for a work environment?"

I told her, "No." She gets visibly upset, leaning back in her chair and eyeballing me.

She said, "Do you hand-wash your clothes?"

I said, "No, I let Shout do the job." (Referring to the stain remover product.)

I'm thinking. *Are you going to call somebody in here?* She was freaking me out.

Finally, her expression revealed an "aha" moment, and she asked, "Have you ever been on dialysis?"

I replied, "Yes, for three years."

She slapped the table and said, "I was about ready to call security." She sighed a sigh of relief for me.

I asked her why, and she said, "You have no fingerprints."

Dialysis had worn away that part of me. Dialysis breaks your body down in ways that are difficult to imagine. When I go through TSA and they ask for fingerprints, I tell them, "You'll have to scan my eyes because there's nothing to scan on the ends of my fingers."

It was more than just an awkward moment for me. It was a reflection of what my body had endured, the way dialysis had stripped away layers of who I was—physically, emotionally, and spiritually.

At every step of my dialysis journey, I had a choice—to let this break me or to keep holding on. This became a recurring theme in my journey: choosing to stay and fight when everything seemed to say, "Let go."

THE BREAKING POINT

Maybe you imagine dialysis as just a medical treatment, but for me, it was starting over every day and every moment. Each appointment became a date with grief. Repeatedly, I grieved the life I used to know and experienced the loss again and again of who I was. The pain was relentless, and there were times I faced a darkness so deep that I could feel the weight of death as a choice I could make.

At one point in fighting to make my way back through that depression, I knew that I could leave earth. I could check out because the torment of staying alive and the exhaustion from what it took from me to keep hanging in there to stay alive was unbearable at times.

Sitting there for hours during dialysis, I listened to various military stories. I learned much about Navy SEALs.

Navy SEALs must pass a test—an exercise where you are taken to the bottom of a very deep pool and have only seconds to take control and not panic. If you panic, you would immediately fail. However, if you calm yourself first, work the problem, and finish your task before you surface the water, you will pass and become a SEAL. It all had to do with giving up "self."

As a SEAL, you:

- Prefer your SEAL teammate over your own life.
- Place the mission before your life.
- Rend yourself of any form of fear.
- Rid yourself of any form of losing self-control.

At the bottom of the pool, they yank your mask off your face, and you have a split second to decide: *Am I going to sit here in all this water?* You must focus your thoughts.

That represents almost every stage of my life. I had to realize my salvation gave me a bigger picture—it was called wholeness. *I'm going to be healed of this. I'm whole.* It's every day, living second by second, not panicking, not freaking out, but trusting God. He is the most trustworthy Being on this planet.

Who else are you going to trust more? Who else is more trustworthy than His Word? It means ridding yourself of all the natural things, fears, doubts, concerns, and what-ifs, and when you can genuinely latch onto that, the hard part is getting past the mental state of all these things. That's when you hit that revelation and become fully persuaded. Once you get to know Him and have revelation knowledge of Him, you start to have revelation knowledge of yourself and the purpose of who He created you to be.

Back to the understanding of the Navy SEALs. While being underwater, they have a choice to win or lose. Fight and maintain composure, or succumb to the pressures of fear and suffocation.

The process of dialysis and the toll it took on my physical, mental, and emotional state brought about many questions. There is a place of numbness when constant pain and the mental battle of life versus death are right in front of you.

There was a point in my life, especially through dialysis, when I started looking at those around me. They were living life to the fullest, being with friends, all while I was in my dialysis chair. This was a hard place to be. Feelings of loneliness and being left behind tried to take over.

That's when I started thinking about my life and the moments when I felt like I had a choice—whether to stay or to leave. There were times during my dialysis when I felt myself slipping, like I could choose to go. It wasn't just physical; it was spiritual, too. I knew that I was at a point where I could choose whether to keep fighting or to let go. Like a SEAL's decision during the difficult underwater test—the decision to give in to this or stay and get through it.

At some moments in those dialysis sessions, I was right on the edge. My body wasn't keeping up with the machines, and it felt like I was slipping in and out of reality. It was so hazy, and I knew I might not make it through if I returned for another session. The choice was laid out before me—stay or leave. I had a deep sense that I could choose either one.

I need to be clear that I was never suicidal when I say I had a choice whether to stay or go. What I mean is that I could choose to give in to the treatments and the wearing down of my body or rise in faith and keep declaring my healing.

I had moments during dialysis when the pain became so loud in my ears, like an unbearable pressure that wouldn't let go. It's like a panic attack—you feel the pain spiraling out of control, and if you don't grab hold of it, it will overwhelm you. I knew that feeling all too well. The pain, exhaustion, and constant trips to dialysis—it was all starting to unravel me to the point where I didn't know if I could hold on.

Even going to God's Word and listening to another preaching message at one point felt tormenting. I was angry because I wasn't seeing anything change. The pain didn't stop, and I was still fighting the same battle every day. It was like the spiritual and physical exhaustion were coming together, and I was on the edge, wondering if I could keep going.

I say all this because I want others to know the strength of staying. Sometimes, the most courageous decision is to keep fighting, even when every part of you is tired. The easy way out often tempts us, but there is a deeper purpose to staying—loving those around us, trusting God, and believing that our story isn't finished yet.

THE CONVERSATION I NEVER WANTED TO HAVE

One of the hardest moments came when I talked to my husband, Joseph. We were standing in the middle of our bedroom, face to face, holding hands. I told him, "I love you," he looked at me, confused like he could sense that I was about to say something heavy. He was trying to guess, thinking maybe the doctor had given me some news or there was something else to work through, as we always did. But he had no idea what I was about to tell him.

I said, "If I die..." and at that moment, his head tilted. He asked me, "What are you saying right now?" I continued, "I want you to find someone who will make you happy. Someone who will take care of you." I needed to know that if I didn't make it, Joseph would be okay and that he'd find someone to help him and our kids move forward.

I said, "You need to find a woman who loves God and will help our daughter grow into the woman she's meant to be. She also needs to be someone who will be patient with Danny, someone who understands his challenges. But most importantly, I want you to find someone who will love you, baby you, and be there for you in the way you need."

At that point, Joseph couldn't hold back anymore. "Don't you say that to me," he told me, with tears in his eyes. "Don't you check out on me." But I looked back at him, thinking *I could go. I could be gone tomorrow, and this pain, this fight, would be over.*

It wasn't just me who was exhausted. Joseph was worn out, too. The weight of caretaking—especially for someone as sick as I was—was crushing him.

It reminded me of people with Alzheimer's, how they don't fully grasp their condition, so they aren't aware of the emotional toll it takes on their caregivers. Joseph felt every bit of the weight. He was carrying the stress of it all—caring for me, raising two young kids, running a ministry, traveling all over the country. I could see it in him. His face was gaunt, his body worn down.

HANG ON A LITTLE LONGER

I'll never forget Valentine's Day that year. I had to go in for yet another port replacement surgery, and the fear gripped me again. I'd woken up during the last surgery, and my fight-or-flight response was off the charts.

I sat down in the waiting room, terrified before the surgery. Then, out of nowhere, I heard Andrew Wommack's voice on the TV say, "Hi, I'm Andrew Wommack, and this is *The Gospel Truth*." At that moment, the Holy Spirit gently told me, "Just hang in there a little bit longer." It wasn't the grand miracles that kept me going—it was those small reminders of His presence.

God's presence is often found in the small, everyday moments. It could be a comforting word, a familiar voice, or a peaceful thought. We don't always need grand miracles to know He is there; we need open hearts to see the quiet ways He holds us.

I kept receiving the constant message: "Hang on a little longer." But in that conversation with Joseph, he told me, "We are not giving up. We are going to beat this." Still, I knew how much it was wearing him down. The stress of keeping our family, our ministry, and me together had taken its toll on him in ways I couldn't ignore. It was a conversation neither of us wanted to have, but it was real.

Through the place of giving up or pressing through, it is in that full circle where you return to trust. It's where you trust God so deeply that you become convinced in daily life matters when you're so filled with Him, and then it grows immensely from within you. It's genuinely you. Not only do you trust Him, but you also begin to trust Him in every circumstance. They can throw anything at you, and you trust Him.

You can say, *I know that the presence of God is speaking to me to go in this direction.* You truly do move to a heavenly reality. You are living an eternal life now. You're not concerned about all these things that aren't going to exist at some point. You have to step out of the physical and know Him like I did when He held me in His hands. I knew Him. I didn't have to say or think it, but He was with me and in me.

Through everything I was feeling and thinking, I chose to stay. I chose to endure the pain because of my children, because of Joseph. The thought of them kept me going, even though the pain of staying was almost too much to bear.

WARFARE WITH THE SPIRIT OF DEATH

Joseph and I were no strangers to spiritual battles, either. One night, Joseph woke up in the middle of the night and saw an entity at the end of our bed. It stood about 7 feet tall and wore a black hood. A spirit of death stood there watching us sleep. This was around the time when I wanted to give up.

Joseph sat up and said, "I bind you in Jesus' name, and I plead the blood over my family." Then he disregarded it and pretended it was nothing. In his unwavering faith, Joseph rebuked it in Jesus' name, turned over, and returned to sleep. He refused to let fear or darkness have any power in our home.

It's just like the devil to try to bring fear when people are in a fragile state. I'm so thankful that Joseph didn't give any thought to that entity standing over me, trying to intimidate me. Joseph knew he had more authority in his little finger than any 7-foot-tall spirit, so he didn't give any attention to the figure standing there. Jesus has given all believers this authority, and through His name and blood, we have the power to defeat the devil.

Sometimes during spiritual warfare, the best thing we can do is stand firm and refuse to give fear any room. When we use

Jesus' name as our authority, we remind ourselves and the enemy that we are children of God and that fear has no place in our lives. "For God has not given us a spirit of fear, but of power and of love and of a sound mind" (2 Timothy 1:7 NKJV).

My time in dialysis produced some incredible ministry moments, but there were also some dark encounters. One was with my dialysis doctor, Dr. C. He was a "head case," as I like to put it—analytical, almost too much in his head. Then there was Dr. G., a doctor from India.

One night, early on in my dialysis journey, Dr. G. came in while I was having a catheter put in my shoulder. I sensed this strange spiritual heaviness around him, and then I saw something demonic flash from his eyes. He looked at me and said, "Oh no, we'll have you on dialysis soon." It wasn't just a comment; it felt like a declaration. "See, I told you we'd get you in here." The way he said it was almost like a dark spirit spoke through him. I could feel it.

At that moment, I was alone and had no one to confirm what I saw, but I knew what had just happened. Then he just smiled and said, "Okay, Heather. Well, we're here for you if you need anything." His whole demeanor shifted, but I knew what I had seen. It was such a demonic moment, and it rattled me.

SERVING OTHERS THROUGH THE PAIN

It wasn't just about surviving. God gave me opportunities to minister to others, even in that dialysis chair. There was a chaplain who came for treatment, and she eventually decided she wasn't coming back. She told me, "This is my last time. I'm too tired." Before she left, I led her in prayer, and she accepted Jesus. We walked out together, and I knew I would never see her again. I could tell she had settled it—she was ready to go.

Pain can be a place where God uses us the most. Even when weak, He allowed me to speak life to others. It taught me that suffering doesn't have to be meaningless—it can be a place where we find purpose and can still reach out and impact those around us.

Dialysis is a form of torture. There's no other way to describe it. If you are not a candidate for transplant, it is a prison sentence. The question becomes, "What is your prison sentence?" Three years, five years, eight years. It's not usually any longer than that. The physical toll, the exhaustion—it wears you down until there's almost nothing left.

I met all kinds of people there—like the guy we called "Thirsty Thursday's Guy." He would come in completely drunk, using dialysis to detox his body of up to twenty pounds of fluid. Some people might judge that, but honestly, I understood. The nurses understood, too. They knew that a little happiness was worth it for some people, even if it wasn't healthy or was a false happiness.

Everyone's journey looks different, and pain affects people in ways we might not fully understand. One day, a man decided he'd had enough. He pulled out his tubes, and his blood started pumping out, spraying everywhere. The heart is so strong—it just kept pushing, even as he tried to end his life.

I could hear the sound of death, which is something I will never forget. I was praying in the Spirit, hoping he'd make it. Joseph came in right behind the paramedics, looking at me like he couldn't believe what he saw. But that was the reality of it. It was raw, brutal, and heartbreaking.

The human heart is resilient. Physically, it fights to keep us alive, and spiritually, it can endure incredible pain. God created us with a strength that we often don't realize until we're in the middle of a battle. Because of that, we can keep pushing forward, even when everything seems impossible.

"YOU'RE DOING A GOOD JOB"

Just moments before entering that horrible scene, Joseph had a powerful moment with God. He had been sitting outside in the parking lot in his truck, feeling the exhaustion of everything—the ministry, our family, the relentless pace. Suddenly, God filled the truck with His presence. Joseph heard God say, "I just want to look at you," like a dad would. And then He said, "You're doing a good job. You're going to be okay."

God's encouragement can give us the strength to keep going.

Hearing that affirmation broke him. God's presence was so strong that Joseph couldn't turn his head; it was like God was beside him, comforting him.

God knows exactly when we need encouragement. Sometimes, amid our exhaustion, all we need is to hear Him say, "You're doing a good job." He sees our struggles and understands the weight we carry. God's encouragement can give us the strength to keep going, even when we feel we have nothing left to give.

Then God's presence began to lift, and Joseph heard sirens and first responders entering the building where I was. He followed them to the scene where this man was trying to end his pain.

THE ANSWER = JESUS

I had a lot of moments when I got to share Jesus with others, even my dialysis doctor. Dr. C. was a cerebral, very analytical man. He couldn't understand why I was still alive, how I was managing without falling apart.

He would look at me and say things such as, "How are you not dead right now?"

I'd smile and say, "Jesus."

But he couldn't grasp that there was a spiritual side to my situation. He'd roll his eyes a little and ask, "But really, what are you eating? What was your diet like?" He couldn't comprehend that faith could play a part in my survival.

He was young, maybe that was part of it, but he was so focused on the science. He'd ask, "Were you drinking just thimbles of water? How did you calculate your output?" He kept getting more cerebral, and I kept saying, "Jesus, Dr. C., Jesus."

But then something shifted. I remember looking at him and saying, "Your daughter is struggling right now, and this is what she's going through. Jesus wants to help her in this area. And your wife, she's having a hard time, and a lot of it has to do with your job. Your family needs you, but you're pulling 12-hour shifts because you think that's what you have to do as a husband and provider." I started naming specific issues with his family, things that only God could reveal to me.

His face changed. "How do you know that?" he asked. And I said, "Jesus. He talks to me, and I listen. This isn't about religion but a relationship with the living God. He's real, and He speaks to me all the time."

I asked if I could pray for him, and as soon as I started, he broke down in tears. This logical, put-together man was completely undone as I prayed for life, peace, and encouragement for him and his family. He admitted, "I've never known anything like this before."

We kept in touch for a while after I had my transplant. I'd send him holiday texts, and he'd respond politely, wishing my family well. Eventually, our communication just tapered off, but it was clear that something had shifted in him.

I wanted him to know the real Jesus, not just an idea or something to turn to on holidays. I wanted him to encounter the living God who speaks and heals, and I tried to show him that day.

God's love can touch even the most unreachable. It wasn't about me—it was about God using my pain to reach someone else. Sometimes, in our weakest moments, God can use us as a light to those searching, even when they don't realize it.

CHOOSING TO STAY

Looking back, I realize I faced death many times. I can't count the times I could have let go. There were moments when I felt the pain so intensely that I just wanted it all to end and for my body to succumb to its decline until death arrived. Yet God reminded me that staying wasn't just about enduring suffering—it was about the impact my life could have on others, especially my family.

Facing death brought a strange sense of peace when I trusted in God's sovereignty. Knowing that I could choose to stay or go and that God would still love me either way set me free.

If you find yourself walking through a similar valley, please know God's love is unwavering, and even when you're at the edge of giving up, His grace is sufficient. It is okay to be honest about your pain, but there is beauty in choosing to stay and fight for the people you love and for the purpose God has for you.

And that's why I chose to stay. Because God is faithful, and He isn't finished with me yet. God was there in every moment—whether it was a reminder through a TV broadcast, Joseph's unwavering support, or the chance to pray with someone who needed hope.

For me, the strength of the human spirit, empowered by faith, is one of the most amazing things God created. We are not just surviving—we are here to fulfill a purpose, His purpose. When we lean into that purpose and trust that God has plans far beyond our understanding, we find the strength to keep going, even in our darkest days.

In choosing to stay, I discovered a strength I never knew I had—a strength in God's faithfulness and His plans for my life. I hope you can find the courage to make the same choice, knowing that your story is far from over.

7

THE ANSWER KEY

I've heard that when someone goes to heaven, they often return with a message or takeaway for life. For me, that's precisely what happened. Many years later, after my time in God's hands, the Holy Spirit said, "I gave you an answer key to help you navigate through future events that will happen to you." I now understand He was speaking about everything from being assaulted as a teen (a form of trafficking), to situations with my children, and my personal sickness. Any one of those things could have killed me, but God had a plan.

It's been like having the teacher's answer key during an exam, providing the answers I've needed to get through the most challenging questions. When I talk about the "answer key," I'm referring to the moments when God made it clear what I needed to do to survive. God's hand guided me, giving me the wisdom and courage to take the proper steps at the right time.

For most of my adult life, I have frequently gone back to the near-death experience I had at 14 years old that I shared in the first chapter, where I was sitting in the Father's hands, and He repeatedly reminded me, "Heather. Everything's going to be okay; I have you in My hands. It's time for you to go now."

That answer key has guided me through near-death experiences, spiritual battles, and, ultimately, into a deeper relationship with God.

THE NIGHT EVERYTHING CHANGED

One night in downtown Minneapolis became a significant turning point in my life. I had been struggling with severe blood clots, and the Holy Spirit made it clear to me that I needed to attend a prayer meeting at the convention center downtown. But the decision to go wasn't easy.

I felt like I was being pulled in two directions. On the one hand, I knew the importance of my role in the ministry—it was like the grabber line in the opening segment of a TV show, crucial for getting people's hearts ready for what was to come. I had to shake myself because our training to be accountable and reliable was so strong in the ministry we served.

On the other hand, I knew deep in my heart that I had to attend that prayer meeting. The pressure was immense, and I felt the weight pressing down on me as I drove away, leaving the ministry and my duties in the capable hands I'd delegated them to for that evening.

Fear gripped me as the weight of my decision sank in. It was getting dark, and I had always been taught that young women should never venture downtown alone at night. Yet there I was, clutching my printed MapQuest directions, preparing to drive into the heart of the city. For 17 years, I had served faithfully at my parents' ministry, and leaving my responsibilities behind felt like a betrayal. But deep in my heart, I knew I had to go.

My stomach and head swirled as I pulled up to the front doors. I exited the car and changed seats with Joseph to take the car downtown. I slid into the driver's seat and thought, *What am I doing? But I know I need to go!*

PUSHING THROUGH THE CROWD

Fear, doubt, and unbelief swirled around me as I drove. I kept thinking, *Will I receive prayer from Andrew Wommack? Should I turn the car around?* But I kept pushing myself forward. I was desperate—like the woman who pushed through the crowd to touch Jesus' garment for healing (Luke 8:43-48). I knew I needed the message that would be preached that night. Even if it didn't lead to total healing, I believed it would strengthen my faith and sustain me for whatever came next.

I thought of Mary Magdalene, searching for Jesus at the tomb, driven by a deep need to find the answer. She was desperate, searching to understand what had happened. She was so overwhelmed that she didn't even recognize Jesus at first, mistaking Him for the gardener. But her heart cried, "Where have you laid my Lord? Where is He?"

When we search for answers with all our hearts, Jesus is ready to reveal Himself to us.

Mary's heart was so stirred for Him that she placed a demand on Jesus without even realizing it. Her love for Him drew Him to her. Even as the heavens rejoiced in His victory over death, hell, and the grave, Jesus paused in His glorious ascent to speak to her and call her by name (John 20:11-18).

In our moments of deepest need, when we're searching for answers with all our hearts, Jesus is ready to reveal Himself to us.

Like Mary, I was so focused on my search, so burdened by the weight of obedience, that I didn't see that Jesus was already with me, working things out behind the scenes. In those moments of raw, honest searching, He speaks our name, reminding us that He's been with us all along, guiding us through the weight of obedience, and leading us to the answers we desperately seek.

A half-hour after the meeting ended, Andrew announced they were not going to have a corporate prayer. He apologized for the short staffing and said he needed to go. I silently said, "Holy Spirit, You told me, 'You have to go to this meeting. You're going to die if you don't.'" So, I waited.

Andrew was supposedly already gone, but about half an hour later, as I was talking to a woman, he suddenly emerged from behind the curtain.

As I walked up to Andrew, all the fear and doubt I'd been wrestling with came to the surface. I had watched him for years and knew him to be no-nonsense and to the point. But at that moment, all I could manage to say was, "I have two days," before breaking into uncontrollable sobs. Everything poured out—tears, raw emotion, all of it. I was a mess, and part of me couldn't help but think, *Where are the ushers with the Kleenex box?*

It's funny how your brain can do several things at once. Even as I was sobbing, part of me was horrified at how I must have looked—streaming tears and my nose running. But I had to shake it off. I needed healing more than I needed to look composed. The enemy tried to distract me in that moment of embarrassment with how much of a mess I was instead of focusing on the purpose of why I was there.

Andrew laid hands on me, but then he pulled back, and I remember him saying, "You do have some sickness going on, but it's more than that...this is demonic oppression." I had never heard him speak about demonic things regarding sickness, but as I stood in front of him, I knew he was right. My husband and I had been ministering in a community dealing with some heavy spiritual darkness, and the attacks we were facing suddenly made sense in light of what Andrew was saying.

He began to pray and commanded healing in my throat and neck. I felt something shift in my spirit, and I knew I had to hold on to that moment as if my life depended on it—because it did.

Someone finally brought me some Kleenex (thank You, Holy Spirit), and I cleaned myself up as best I could. As I walked out of the convention center, I felt a deep peace. God told me again, "Everything's going to be okay."

FROM TRANSACTIONAL FAITH TO FAITH ROOTED IN LOVE

That night marked a significant shift in my spiritual journey. Until then, I had approached faith transactionally—praying, fasting, and reading the Bible, expecting God to respond based on my actions. I believed that He had to heal me if I did everything right. However, that mindset left me frustrated and spiritually drained.

I realized that I had been treating my relationship with God like a series of transactions—*if I do this, He'll do that.* But that night in Minneapolis, I began to understand that my faith needed more than just following rules. It had to become a deeper, abiding love for God. That night, the Holy Spirit whispered, "Get to know Me. Don't just know about Me—fall in love with Me for real."

A spiritual breakthrough came when I stopped relying on my efforts and truly surrendered to God's love.

That's when things started to change. As I moved from a transactional faith to one rooted in love, I began to see healing manifest in my life. It wasn't just believing that God *could heal me;* it was knowing *He already had,* and aligning my life with that truth.

I often think about this shift in my faith like a "runner's high." I trained a lot when I was younger—I even trained for a triathlon. I'd heard people talk about "runner's high," but I never understood what they meant until I experienced it on race day. Only when I pushed myself to the absolute limit did I finally feel that euphoric rush, that sense of crossing over into something greater.

In the same way, my spiritual breakthrough came when I pushed past my limits—when I stopped relying on my efforts and truly surrendered to God's love. It was like I had been running the race of faith with everything I had, and finally, I crossed over into that place where faith, hope, and love converged.

THE BATTLE OF MENTAL FORTITUDE AND PERSEVERANCE

This journey wasn't just about a single moment of breakthrough. It was a battle of mental fortitude and perseverance—a fight I had to keep engaging in daily. The battle in the mind is where the enemy will try to wear you down, often with discouragement, which comes when you're not seeing any change in the circumstances you are fighting for. This is a tactic the devil uses to bring you down so that you will quit.

After that night in Minneapolis, I had to endure for two more days, clinging to the truth that I was healed, even when my circumstances screamed otherwise. I had to hang on and refuse to allow anything into my ears through conversation and into my heart that would take away the deposit I received through the prayer spoken over me.

This required me to be very assiduous in my faith, being fully persuaded that I was healed the moment I received prayer. Hanging on to it, I did not allow any inner or outside influence to sway me otherwise because every time I bent forward, the blood clots in my throat would choke me, making it hard to breathe. I fought to disesteem every symptom, telling myself 1,000 times over, "I am healed, and I did receive healing the moment hands were laid on me."

Every minute was a game of tug-of-war, with my faith on one side and the reality of my circumstances on the other. The Holy Spirit was a coach on the sidelines, shouting encouragement from God's Word: "This is possible! You can do it! You have to do it! I can't do it for you!"

I knew something had changed when I woke up on the morning of my scan. As I washed my face and ran my hands down my neck, I gasped—the lumps were gone, and my neck was completely smooth. I tried leaning forward and bending every which way, but nothing happened. I no longer choked or gasped for breath.

I ran to my husband, Joseph, yelling, "I'm healed, I'm healed, I'm healed!" We celebrated together, knowing that if God could do this, He could also take care of everything else.

At the clinic, the doctors looked at me like I was wasting their time. They went through with the scan anyway, and the results confirmed what I already knew—there were no blood clots in my throat anymore. I was completely healed. But this victory didn't come without a fight. It required mental toughness and perseverance that I had never experienced before.

LOVE'S REVELATION AND THE FINISHED WORK OF JESUS

Through all this, I learned that true healing and breakthroughs require more than knowing scripture or performing religious duties. They require aligning yourself with God's finished work and truly understanding the depth of His love for you. When I finally understood this, I saw the breakthrough I had longed for.

This new revelation wasn't just about healing, either. I applied the same mentality to other areas of my life—relationships, finances, and ministry. I realized everything I needed was already provided for in my covenant with Jesus. It was up to me to align myself with that truth, stand firm in my faith, and refuse to give up until I saw the manifestation of God's promises in my life.

When we act in faith, we invite the supernatural power of God to move in our circumstances.

One of the things that helped me through this process was the teaching I had received over the years, particularly a message from Rick Renner about the "Tormentor." He described how the enemy comes to beat you down to the point where you're almost dead but leaves just enough life in you to keep you going, only to come back and beat you down again. That's how sickness works—it tries to wear you down over time.

Rick's message reminded me that I have the authority, in Jesus' name, to kick anything out of my life, whether sickness, fear, or any other form of attack. I had to stand up, take authority, and refuse to let the enemy keep me down.

INVITE THE SUPERNATURAL POWER OF GOD

Another message that resonated deeply with me was from my husband, who preached "How to Get a Supernatural Reaction." I realized that I needed to act based on my faith, aligning myself with what God had already done. I began to see that this principle applied to healing in every area of my life.

KIDNEY TRANSPLANT

Finally, the miracle came—I received a kidney transplant. It was incredible, but the real miracle was what God had done in my heart during those years of struggle. He had taught me to trust and love Him completely and to rest in His promises.

He had brought me to a place of complete trust and surrender. He had shown me that His presence was what I needed, which gave me peace—far more than any physical healing ever could. The transplant was a new beginning, but my relationship with God was the true gift.

This journey taught me that healing isn't just about the physical body. While the transplant gave me a new physical lease on life, my relationship with God gave me something far more valuable—a deep and abiding peace that surpassed all understanding. Healing is about the heart, mind, and spirit. It's about finding our true refuge in God's presence and knowing Him in the deepest way possible.

DON'T GIVE UP

To anyone facing similar challenges, I want to encourage you to persevere. Don't give up, even when the battle seems overwhelming. Hold on to the truth of God's Word, stand firm in your faith, and refuse to let go until you see the manifestation of His promises in your life. It may sometimes feel like a wrestling match, but remember that you are not alone—God is with you, and His love is more powerful than any challenge you face. Just like Jacob wrestled with God and prevailed (Genesis 32:22-32), you can overcome challenges by holding fast to God's promises and never letting go.

If you're in a moment of pressing through, I know the mind and body can get tired. In these moments, you need to have the most compassion for yourself. You need to lay your hands on yourself and speak peace over your mind, heart, emotions, and body.

God gave me the answer key: Push through the crowd, persevere through the challenges, and hold fast to His promises. Get to know Him, and He will direct you through every situation the enemy brings.

Remember, God's love surrounds you and will carry you through every step of the journey.

> *For I know the thoughts that I think toward you, says the Lord, thoughts of peace and not of evil, to give you a future and a hope. Then you will call upon Me and go and pray to Me, and I will listen to you. And you will seek Me and find Me, when*

you search for Me with all your heart. I will be found by you, says the Lord....

—Jeremiah 29:11-14 NKJV

8

THE INTERSECTION OF MIRACLES AND HEALING

Sometimes in life, we face impossible situations—places where we either give up or hang on by a thread. My story is a mix of miracles and healing, two very different experiences that have shaped my journey through illness, faith, and trust in God. In this chapter, I share my moments of supernatural intervention and the daily challenges of simply staying alive.

Looking back on my experiences in the supernatural, I see my story fall into two categories: the miraculous and the healing process. The miraculous part includes moments like dying and seeing the Lord—powerful, immediate encounters with His presence. But there's also the day-in, day-out healing process where I had to trust God, not just once but repeatedly.

I told you about being in the middle of a dialysis session when I heard the Holy Spirit speak to me. I was hooked on the machine and knew it was God. I knew it was time to go.

I had been in that chair for less than 30 minutes, feeling the adrenaline rush that always comes at the start of treatment. That first rush would spike for about 45 minutes, and I would eventually fall asleep from exhaustion. But this time, something felt different.

GOD'S VOICE

People often ask me, "How did you know it was God's voice? Was it like a booming voice from heaven?" Honestly, it wasn't anything like that.

God's voice was so clear. That's not something you imagine or tell yourself lightly. It was an inner knowing, and I had learned to recognize it through years of trusting Him. It wasn't an audible voice, but it felt as clear as someone speaking to me. Over time, I learned to discern His voice through the scriptures and quiet moments of prayer. That knowing developed after a year of intentionally filling myself with God's promises, especially what the Bible says about healing.

I wasn't just sitting at home with all the time in the world to soak in the Word of God. Life continued around me—I needed to take care of kids and get them to school, and daily tasks demanded my attention. It was exhausting. I constantly had to choose between being a mother and a patient, and there were so many days when I just wanted to give up.

I had dialysis runs starting at 5 a.m. that lasted almost four hours, which meant rushing to get my kids to school right afterward, often resulting in them arriving late. I remember the parent-teacher conferences about their tardiness and how I struggled to balance everything.

Sometimes I'd switch to the second shift but often arrive late, cutting into my treatment time, which I could never get back. The staff told me, "You can't keep cutting your sessions short." It was a constant battle between survival and living.

Like any relationship, building trust with God is an investment.

Life didn't pause because of my health. Despite the chaos, I made time for God's Word because I had to—it was a matter of life and death. I needed to hear God's voice to survive.

I've said this, but it bears repeating—healing doesn't always happen instantly. Sometimes, it's a process that requires patience, resilience, and trust in God's timing. While we often pray for miracles, we should also learn to value the slower, daily work of healing God does in our lives. Both are expressions of His love, requiring us to lean on Him.

Learning to hear God's voice takes effort, time, practice, and intimacy with Him. Immersing myself in God's Word allowed me to discern His voice in critical moments. Building trust with God is an investment, just like any relationship. If you want to hear Him in the big moments, you must start by listening in the small ones.

Even when we are facing our crises, life's responsibilities don't stop. In these moments God's grace becomes most evident. I learned His strength was sufficient for me, helping me do what

I couldn't do alone. If you're feeling overwhelmed by everything you have to carry, you don't have to do it all perfectly. God will carry you through. While hearing God's voice guided me spiritually, there were practical challenges I faced every day.

GOD'S PROMPTING

Dialysis itself was brutal. After the adrenaline rush I mentioned that comes in the first 45 minutes, my body gave in to exhaustion. I sat in a chair for almost four hours, with strangers next to me lined up against the wall with no privacy—nothing but chairs, machines, and people sharing this strange, painful journey.

The more experienced patients would offer tips to the new ones. "Bring your favorite blanket and socks," they'd say. "You'll get cold." It wasn't the nurses; we were helping each other get through it. We were all in the same boat, facing the same struggles, and that built a strange sense of community. I met people I never would have known otherwise, like the man from India who sat next to me. He had a strong accent, and we often talked about God. He believed there were many ways to God, but I was firm. I would tell him, "No, there's only one way." It was so important to share what I knew with him because, in the end, if he didn't know Jesus, he wouldn't make it to heaven. Many deep conversations stayed with me even after he was gone.

Suffering has a way of bringing people together and creating unexpected bonds. The room was lined with chairs, each paired with a machine, and we faced each other. I remember watching people next to me—some swollen with fluid, others who had lost limbs to diabetes. For the new patients, it was hard, and we all knew it.

In those dialysis chairs, we became advocates for one another, forming a community that sustained us in the hardest moments.

The process was taxing, and it was clear how much it took from everyone. In those dialysis chairs, we weren't just patients—we became advocates for one another, forming a community that sustained us in the hardest moments. We were all in it together, facing our battles. We supported each other, and that sense of community was a lifeline. It reminded me that we're not meant to go through hardships alone—God designed us to lean on each other. When we choose to share our heartaches, we find strength and hope.

I lost friends during that time—people whose lives ended while I was still there. It was hard because we were sharing our fears and stories every day, and then, suddenly, they just weren't there anymore.

I'll never forget the day I came in, and my friend from India wasn't there. I immediately noticed the flowers at the nurses' station. His family had sent them to thank the staff for caring for him, and it broke my heart. In that room, we didn't just share our struggles—we also shared our losses. It taught me how important it is to cherish every moment with the people God brings into my life because we never know how much time we have.

LIFE AND DEATH DECISIONS

When it was my turn to face a critical decision, I had to rely on the Holy Spirit for guidance. After my kidney transplant, I felt my body failing again, and at a follow-up appointment, the doctors told me I had half the amount of blood I needed.

I was barely conscious; it took everything I had to hold on to his voice!

In the middle of a snowstorm—not long after they gave me that news—Joseph had to rush me to the Heart Health Center. I remember slumping over in the car, feeling myself fading. Joseph pushed me through the snow in a wheelchair, yelling, "Hang on, Heather! Just a little longer."

I was barely conscious. Thank God he had a new truck because the snowbank at the end of our driveway stood taller than my desk. He was able to drive up and over it. It took everything I had to stay awake and hold on to his voice!

When we got there, they checked my blood. My hemoglobin was at five. I had half the blood I needed in my body, and they told me, "If we have to operate, you'll die. You don't have enough blood to survive a surgery."

They wanted to give me a blood transfusion, and all I could think of was the warning I'd been given. My friend from India had warned, "If they offer you a blood transfusion, don't take it. It could change your blood and make you ineligible for a transplant." He spoke from experience—he'd had a kidney transplant, and after a transfusion, his body rejected it. He ended up back in that chair for life. That thought terrified me, and I wasn't ready to make the decision lightly.

I was weak, had no color in my face, and my body was barely holding on. The doctors explained that if my organs started to shut down, there was nothing they could do to save me. They brought in specialists, and I asked the doctors every question I could think of. I needed to know if this was the right choice.

Joseph and I prayed, considered our options, and asked God for wisdom. After two days of praying, we decided I should have the transfusion. I felt peace about it and knew that was God's answer. It was still terrifying. I ended up receiving multiple bags of blood, and I had to be my own advocate the whole time.

God gives us the wisdom to speak up when necessary.

This was the time they had placed a blood pressure cuff over my IV needle, and every time it squeezed, it felt like my arm was on fire. I begged them to move it to my leg. When you're desperate, you get creative. You learn to speak up for yourself, and I did. Eventually, they moved it, and I finally got some relief.

Advocating for yourself is crucial, especially when you're vulnerable. No one knows your body like you do, and God gives us the wisdom to speak up when needed. In times of hardship, it's vital to trust the instincts God has placed in you and fight for the care you need.

I could only trust God's guidance in those moments of life and death. I knew that my life depended on making the right decision; the only way I could do that was by depending on God's wisdom.

Faith isn't just about trusting God in the abstract—it's about bringing every choice, fear, and question to Him.

HEALING AND PHYSICAL TOUCH

God's help can come through the most unexpected people. One day, shortly after the transfusion, a woman came in to offer massage therapy. She wasn't a believer, but she had a gift. The moment she laid her hands on me, I felt my body respond. It felt like stepping into sunlight after a long winter—my whole body came alive again. God used her touch to make a huge difference in my recovery.

He can use anyone—whether they know Him or not—to bring comfort and healing. We must remain open to receiving His blessings, even when they come from places we wouldn't have considered or anticipated. God works in mysterious ways.

Sometimes He sends the right person at the right time, even if they don't share our faith.

Joy can break through the pain even when life feels unbearable.

I must mention one of the most significant people who helped me: Nurse M.B. She had the best bedside manner and always found ways to make me laugh. She was like Patch Adams, bringing humor into the most challenging moments. She'd come in with medical underwear on her head, making jokes, trying to lift my spirits and make me smile. She'd say, "Time to get dressed!" She made an otherwise humiliating experience bearable. She knew what I needed, not just physically but emotionally, too.

Laughter and joy are powerful tools for healing, even in the darkest times. M.B.'s humor helped me see that joy can break through the pain, even when life feels unbearable. It's okay to let yourself laugh, even when you're struggling. You're not ignoring the seriousness of your situation but embracing the strength joy provides. In those moments, laughter was as much a part of my healing as the medical treatments.

I experienced so many moments of complete vulnerability—times when my body was shutting down, and medical staff had to intervene, leaving me exposed and without dignity. It was humbling and forced me to let go of my pride.

Letting go of pride can open us up to God's grace in a way that nothing else can. Stripped of all dignity, I experienced God's presence the most in those moments of complete surrender. Admitting that we can't do it on our own brings power. It's in our weakness that God's strength becomes most evident, and that's where true healing begins (2 Corinthians 12:9).

When life feels impossible, God gives us the grace to take it one moment at a time.

ONGOING BATTLES

Even as I improved, I struggled. I was prescribed 27 different medications, some multiple times a day, and the pill schedule overwhelmed me at first. I had to be so careful—one mistake could be deadly. It was just one more battle in a long line of battles. I used three large weekly pill organizers to keep track. But I knew each pill was essential to my survival. Prednisone was the worst—it made me feel like I was outside of my mind. At times, it caused me not to recognize myself. But I kept pushing forward.

Looking into the face of overwhelming challenges often requires taking one step at a time. Trying to manage everything at once paralyzed me. Instead, I focused on taking each dose of medication, each small task, one at a time. It's the same in our spiritual journey. When life feels impossible, God gives us the grace to take it one moment at a time. We don't have to know what the future holds—we need to trust Him for what we need today.

One of the hardest parts was the emotional toll the battle I fought took on my relationships. Pain and suffering can test even the strongest relationships. When very sick, it's easy to wear out the people who care about you. Friends and family had already sat with me for hours, prayed over me, and supported me in every way they could. But there came a point where I still needed more, and they didn't have it in them to give. I remember feeling hurt, wondering why they couldn't stay with me just a little longer, why they seemed to be pulling away. But now I see they had already done so much. They were drained, and it wasn't that they didn't care—they had reached their limit. They couldn't fill the deep need that only God could meet.

Expecting others to always be there and understand wasn't fair to them or me. We need compassion for those trying to support us—they're doing their best. We must also learn to bring our deepest needs to God, knowing He is the only One who can truly meet us in our darkest places.

SUPPORT AND COMPASSION

My journey through a kidney transplant gave me deep empathy for others who are suffering. It gave me so much compassion. When I talk to people in pain now, I understand how real it is for them. I understand that sometimes, they can't just "get over it." They need support, love, and patience.

I know what it's like to feel at the end of your rope, to need support, and to feel like you're not getting enough. I also understand that sometimes people can't give anymore, and that's okay. It's where they are. But that's why God has given us medical professionals, nurses, and others who step in when friends and family can't. Their role is vital, and I'm grateful for every one of them.

Sometimes, it's just about hanging on until the breakthrough comes.

God was with me in the miraculous moments—like when I heard His voice telling me to leave dialysis—and in the everyday battles, like managing medications and enduring the pain of treatment. I learned to trust Him, to advocate for myself, and to find strength in His presence.

Healing isn't always immediate, and miracles aren't always dramatic. Sometimes, it's just about hanging on—one more day, one more minute—until the breakthrough comes. God is always faithful and present in those moments, carrying us through. He uses the unexpected people, the moments of laughter, the friends who show up, and even those who can't. He teaches us to be patient with ourselves and others and reminds us that His grace is enough even when we feel exposed and vulnerable.

If you're fighting your own battle, know that God is with you. Whether you need immediate intervention or are walking through the slow recovery process, He sees you and cares. Take it one step at a time, trust Him with the next decision, and know He is faithful to carry you through.

9

WHOLENESS—GETTING TO KNOW HIM

During my journey through dialysis and the kidney transplant, I told you how I cried out to God, and He answered me. He was clear: "Get to know Me. Fall in love with Me for real, to the point that you don't care if you live or die." Part of getting to know Him and trust Him completely leads to wholeness.

God wants you to walk in the fullness of all He has for you. He wants us to understand who we are in Christ. He also desires for us to experience all the power available to us through salvation and how to access the supernatural promises He's made to us in His Word.

Jesus is the standard, the firstborn among many brethren (Romans 8:29). He's our example of how we should act. Nobody will be Jesus, but we must understand that He is the prototype.

Some say, "Well, He had the Holy Spirit in Him beyond measure. He had God living inside Him." Who do you think you have living inside you? The same Holy Spirit. You become a wrecking ball to the kingdom of darkness when you know who you are. You become a terroristic force to darkness and evil—spiritually speaking.

The reason Christians get their minds messed up, get depressed, and lose grip of their purpose is that they don't know who they are. The weakest among us is greater than all the forces of hell. The devil doesn't care that you're a son or daughter of God. He doesn't care that you have all the power and authority. His biggest fear is that one day, you might discover it.

As I've shared, I was sick for years. Doctors kept saying, "Get your affairs in order. Say goodbye to your husband and kids—you're going to die."

After two and a half years of that, I had enough. I got righteous anger inside and said, "I'm not doing this anymore!" I decided either God's Word is true, or it's not. I believe it is. When Jesus said, "It is finished," He meant it (John 19:28-30). The healing was already done. The problem wasn't God—it was a knowledge issue on my part. I had to get past the veil of my five senses and grab hold of what was already mine in the Spirit.

SEVEN PARTS OF SALVATION

The Greek word for salvation, *soteria,* appears 45 times in the New Testament.[1] Salvation (or *soteria*) has seven parts. It means you are:

1. Saved from hell.

1. Soteria: salvation, save, saving, deliver; Strong's #4991; BibleTools; https://www.bibletools.org/index.cfm/fuseaction/Lexicon.show/ID/G4991/soteria.htm; accessed February 11, 2025.

2. Delivered from danger. Psalm 91 and Galatians 1:4 say it is the will of God for you to be delivered from this present, evil age.
3. Preserved. Kept sanctified until you meet the Lord and are made like Him.
4. Provided for through God's economy.
5. Protected.
6. Healed. Healing is progressive. It is like going to the doctor, getting a prescription, and walking it out progressively. Miracles happen suddenly—boom!
7. Made whole, which is miraculous. Wholeness is another category altogether. It's better than the original state.

Look at the ten lepers Jesus healed:

> *And it came to pass, as he went to Jerusalem, that he passed through the midst of Samaria and Galilee. And as he entered into a certain village, there met him ten men that were lepers, which stood afar off: and they lifted up their voices, and said, Jesus, Master, have mercy on us. And when he saw them, he said unto them, Go shew yourselves unto the priests. And it came to pass, that, as they went, they were cleansed.*
>
> *And one of them, when he saw that he was healed, turned back, and with a loud voice glorified God, and fell down on his face at his feet, giving him thanks: and he was a Samaritan. And Jesus*

> *answering said, Were there not ten cleansed? but where are the nine? There are not found that returned to give glory to God, save this stranger. And he said unto him, Arise, go thy way: thy faith hath made thee whole.*
>
> **—Luke 17:11-19 KJV**

Nine walked away healed, but *the one who returned was made whole.* Whatever he was lacking—fingers, toes, whatever—was fully restored!

I learned that sickness is illegal in our bodies. But to access healing, you must be fully persuaded in your heart. Knowing the scriptures mentally is not enough; you must believe them in your spirit. When doctors said I'd die, I laughed because I knew I was already healed.

THE NATURAL AND SPIRITUAL REALMS

Remember I said I had to get past the veil of my five senses and grab hold of what was already mine in the Spirit? The natural is where our five senses operate. The natural comes first, then the spiritual. Many people think the spiritual comes first because it's more spiritual. But 1 Corinthians 15:46 says the natural is first, then the spiritual. That principle applies here.

The spiritual is the greater reality, where everything in salvation is already done.

- *Grace* is what God has done for you.

- *Faith* is what you do to access it.
- The veil I mentioned lies between the two, which are our five senses.

When you step out in faith, you go beyond your five senses. For example, laying hands on the sick is a natural action, but it activates a supernatural reaction. Hebrews 5:14 tells us to exercise our senses to discern between good and evil.

Praying in the Spirit helps us align with God's Word. It bypasses our five senses and puts us into the Spirit. Speaking in tongues is one of the greatest weapons God gave the Church. When you pray in tongues, your mind doesn't understand it, but your spirit is edified. Jude says to build yourself up in your most holy faith by praying in the Spirit (Jude 1:20).

Do you need healing? Do you want everything God has for you through your salvation? If so, here's what you need to do:

- Speak the Word of God out loud. You can't fight thoughts with thoughts; you'll lose every time. I had to speak against the enemy's lies, even in the grocery store. People probably thought I was crazy, but my life depended on it.
- Lay hands on yourself and declare: "These are healing hands. Healing is mine! Right now, in the name of Jesus, I declare healing and wholeness over my body. Pain, leave! Blood cells respond to the blood of Jesus! Bones, nerves, and organs be made whole!"

Pray the Word over your circumstances. Jesus has already won the victory. Everything you need is in Him.

EMBRACE WHOLENESS

As you've learned from reading this book, I've experienced some incredibly difficult seasons—times of deep emotional pain, physical ailments, and overwhelming circumstances. But through it all, God has been faithful. No matter how dark the night is, He's shown me His light is always shining, guiding me toward wholeness.

I had moments when the weight of my circumstances felt unbearable, and I felt like giving up. Yet, in the middle of it all, God reminded me of His presence. He assured me His healing hand was at work, even when I couldn't see it. He restored me in ways I never imagined and fulfilled His purpose through trials I thought I wouldn't survive.

I've seen firsthand how God's Word can transform a situation. Proverbs 4:23 (NKJV) says, "Keep your heart with all diligence, for out of it spring the issues of life." This verse has been a guiding light for me, especially when life gets tough. It's such a powerful command! God tells us to guard our hearts because everything we do flows from them. Our challenges, struggles, and decisions all stem from what's in our hearts.

Here's the beautiful thing: even when life throws its hardest punches, God is right there, helping us to guard our hearts, reminding us of the purpose He has placed within us.

SO, WHAT'S IN YOUR HEART?

Just as I was coming out of a difficult season where I felt overwhelmed by the challenges I faced, Proverbs 4:23 became very real. My husband and I had been through some tough times, and it seemed like everything was hitting us all at once. But in the midst of it all, God reminded me to:

- Keep my heart with all diligence.
- Stay focused on Him.
- Trust in His Word.

God designed each of us with a destiny, but here's a word of caution: Just because God has a purpose for us doesn't mean it will automatically come to pass. We must partner with Him, obey His Word, and guard our hearts against what would try to derail us.

We have to take action and decide to pursue healing and wholeness.

One of the biggest challenges we face is offense. The enemy uses the powerful tool of offense to try and take us off course if we choose to let him. We know that offenses will come, but what is important is how we respond to them.

Offense often starts with a simple thought that, if not addressed, can grow into a negative belief system that affects how we see the world. It can be based on false information, misunderstandings, or even feeling threatened.

While our bodies are designed to heal themselves when we experience a physical injury, our minds and emotions don't work the same way. We have to be intentional about healing our hearts and minds. It doesn't happen automatically. We have to take action and decide to pursue healing and wholeness.

I've had to go through the healing process more times than I can count. There was a time when someone close to me deeply hurt me. The pain was so real and so deep that it felt like it would never go away. But God began to teach me about forgiveness—true, deep forgiveness.

Forgiveness is not just about saying the words, it's about taking action. It's about forgiving, even when the feelings are raw, and the pain is still real. It's about saying out loud, "Lord, I forgive them. I release them." As we continue to say those words, something changes in our hearts. The healing process begins when we trust God to heal our hearts.

FORGIVENESS IS A PROCESS

It usually doesn't happen overnight, and it's not always easy. But it's necessary if we want to live in God's freedom.

Consider forgiveness like letting go of a rope attached to a loud, clanging bell. As long as we keep holding on, the bell keeps ringing, reminding us of the pain. But the moment we let go, it might ring loudly in the beginning, but as you continue to say by faith, "Lord, I forgive, but help me to forgive," the less you will hear the bell ringing. This is a faith action, similar to the father who said, "Lord, I believe, but help my unbelief." The ringing *will* fade until it stops, and you *will* find peace. The key is being brave enough to let go of the rope.

I remember sitting with a couple many years ago, sharing some of the hurts I had experienced in the church. A gentleman we called "Pops" looked at me compassionately and said, "Heather, you've got to forgive." His words were simple, but they carried so much weight. I knew that forgiveness was the key to unlocking the door to my healing, and I decided to start the process that day.

DIFFERENT WAYS HEALING OCCURS

Sometimes healing is a journey that takes time, and we must keep pressing in and trusting God. Other times healing is miraculous and happens in an instant. I've experienced both. When I broke my neck and should have died, God performed a miracle. I walked away, completely healed. That was an instantaneous healing. But I've also walked through long seasons of waiting for healing, where God taught me and grew me. He didn't cause these seasons, but He used them to help me in more ways than I could imagine.

Whether your healing comes instantly or over time, keeping your heart with all diligence is key. Don't let the issues of life take root in your heart. Don't allow offense, fear, or disappointment to dictate your life. Instead, focus on God's promises. Get into His Word and let it fill your heart and mind. That's how you keep your heart with all diligence—by staying rooted in God's Word and His truth.

Jesus is the perfect example of how to do this. When tempted in the wilderness, He combated every temptation with the Word of God. He didn't argue with the devil or try to reason with him.

He said, "It is written" (Matthew 4:1-11; Luke 4:2-14). That's how we overcome—by saying what God has already said in His Word and declaring His truth over our lives.

The enemy doesn't give up easily. Even after Jesus resisted the devil in the wilderness, the scripture says that the devil left Him for a more opportune time. The enemy will try to return, find a weak spot, and see if he can get us to fall. However, we can always overcome if we keep our hearts with all diligence and stay rooted in God's Word.

PURSUE PEACE WITH ALL PEOPLE

Hebrews 12:14 (NKJV) says, "Pursue peace with all people, and holiness, without which no one will see the Lord." Peace is something we have to pursue actively. This pursuit is like hunting it down until you capture it. It's not always easy, especially when hurt or wronged, but it's essential for healing and well-being. When we pursue peace, not only do we find healing, we also create an environment where others can experience God's peace as well. I've learned the meaning of this verse by watching Rick Renner extensively teach it.

If you've been hurt, are struggling with unforgiveness, or are dealing with any emotional pain, I hope you will take the first step toward healing. Make the decision today to forgive, let go of the hurt, and trust God to heal your heart. Speak it out loud: "Lord, I forgive them. I release them." As you do, watch as God begins to bring healing and restoration to your life.

Let me pray for you:

> *Father, in the name of Jesus, I pray for every person reading this today. I ask that You help them to keep their hearts with all diligence, to stay rooted in Your Word, and to trust You in every situation. Lord, I ask for Your healing power to flow into their hearts and minds right now. Help them forgive, let go of any hurt or offense, and walk in the freedom that You have for them. I speak peace over their hearts, minds, and bodies and declare they are whole in Jesus' name. Amen.*

No matter where you are in life, God's purpose for you remains. Trust Him, and let His hands carry you into the fullness of what He has planned.

THREE THINGS TO KNOW

No matter what you're facing, hold on to your faith. God is with you in every trial, shadowy moment, and tear that falls. There have been times when I wondered if God was there and if He truly saw the depth of my pain. Now I know He was always there, faithfully providing a way out, lifting the sadness from my heart, and bringing me His peace.

1. God provides a way out of every trial (1 Corinthians 10:13).

Even when our circumstances don't change immediately, we can rest assured that God is at work. He is present, lifting the heaviness from our hearts and preparing us for His greater plan.

2. He is the Comforter.

Beyond just providing a way out, God is our Comforter amid the storm. Psalm 34:18 (NIV) says, "The Lord is close to the brokenhearted and saves those who are crushed in spirit." When you feel crushed by the weight of your circumstances, know He is near. He longs to bring you peace that surpasses all understanding. He is your refuge in times of trouble, with arms wide open, ready to hold you close.

3. God has a unique plan for your life.

God is not surprised by what you're going through. He's already made a way. While He held me in His hands as a young teen, God revealed to me that He had created me for assignments and a purpose established before the foundation of the world. That's true for you, too. God has a plan for your life—one set in motion long before you were born, and He's working all things together for your good (Romans 8:28).

Even when we can't see it, or life feels chaotic, God is weaving every joy and pain into a beautiful tapestry that reflects His glory. Remember, God's timing often doesn't align with ours. Isaiah 55:8-9 reminds us that His ways and thoughts are higher than ours. When it feels like He is taking too long, trust that His timing is perfect. While you wait, He is preparing you for the blessings to come.

FIVE THINGS TO DO:

1. Engage in prayer, especially when life feels overwhelming.

One of the most powerful tools we have as believers is prayer. Prayer connects us to God's miraculous power and allows Him to work in our lives. Throughout my journey, I've witnessed the power of prayer. I've seen God respond to the simplest, most faith-filled prayers with miracles that defy human understanding.

2. Seek support.

Don't walk through challenges alone. Seek support from God and those around you. Surround yourself with people who will pray with you, stand with you, and believe with you. It's so important not to isolate yourself when you're going through tough times. God designed us to live in community, and there is great strength and healing in the support of fellow believers.

If you feel alone, reach out to a church community or a group of believers who can support you in your healing journey.

Never underestimate the power of a simple prayer—whether yours or someone else's prayer for you. God doesn't need fancy words; He needs your heart. Believe that He is listening, cares for you, and can and will do miracles in your life.

3. Walk in authority.

Whether you're overcoming mental and emotional strongholds or seeking physical healing, remember that God has given you the authority to overcome every obstacle through His power.

In 2 Corinthians 10:4-5, we're reminded that the weapons of our warfare are not of the flesh but have divine power to destroy strongholds. Don't hesitate to call on the name of Jesus and declare His victory over your life.

4. Reflect on your own life.

You've read my story. Now, take a moment to reflect on your own. Where do you need God's healing touch? Where do you need to invite Him into your circumstances? Know that God is attentive to your prayers. He sees you, hears you, and waits for you to turn to Him.

5. Invite God in.

God sees every detail of your life and waits for you to invite Him in. Don't try to carry the weight of your struggles alone. God wants to be involved in every part of your life. Trust Him with your struggles, hopes, and fears. When you invite Him into your circumstances, He'll begin to work in ways you never expected.

I hope you will choose to walk in the fullness of what God has for you today, knowing that victory is already yours through Jesus Christ.

10

FIRED UP AND READY TO FIGHT

We've come to the end of this journey together, but what feels like the end is just the beginning. Throughout this book, we've talked about God's healing, presence, power, and faithfulness. Now it's time to take everything you've learned and let it fuel your fire. This chapter isn't just about wrapping up—it's about stepping into the life of wholeness God has for you with boldness and authority.

Life isn't going to slow down or get easier just because you're ready to move forward. The enemy is still out there, hoping to keep you stuck, doubting, or afraid. But let me remind you: greater is He who is in you than he who is in the world (1 John 4:4). This is your moment to rise, ignite the power of the Holy Spirit inside you, and declare victory in every area of your life.

Don't let what you've learned here stay on the pages of this book. Allow His revelation to come alive in your heart and life. Let's step into this last chapter with confidence and determination, knowing God has equipped you for the fight ahead.

We live in a time where everything around us seems uncertain. The world is loud and chaotic, and the enemy will try to make you feel isolated, weak, and overwhelmed. But guess what?

You're not in this alone, and you're certainly not powerless. No matter where you've come from, whether you've been walking with Jesus for years or just starting, you have power that can't be denied. You carry a strength given to you by God Himself, and that gets me fired up!

Tap into the strength. Refuse to let the enemy have the last word. Remind the enemy who he's dealing with. You are a believer filled with the Holy Spirit, standing in victory because of what Jesus has already done.

JESUS REVEALS HIMSELF TO ANYONE

One of the things that amazes me most about Jesus is how He reveals Himself to people. It's not about their status, background, or past mistakes. Look at the woman at the well (John 4). She wasn't exactly on top of the social ladder. She had five husbands—and in her culture, she would have been shamed and treated as an outcast. People didn't want to be associated with someone like her.

God's purpose for you comes from the potential He placed inside you.

But Jesus didn't care about any of that. He didn't care about her broken past; He cared about her future. He saw something in her that no one else did. When He spoke to her, He didn't bring up her past to condemn her—He brought it up to show her that He *knew* all of her and still chose to reveal Himself to her. Because of that encounter, she became the one to kick off His public ministry.

She didn't just meet Jesus—she ran back to her people and said, "Let me tell you about this man, the Messiah—He's here!" She was the social media post of her day that went viral in the best way possible! She announced the coming of the Savior to a whole town, and because of her, many believed. God's purpose for us isn't based on our past but on what He sees in us, the potential He placed inside us.

LIGHT YOURSELF ON FIRE

If you think you don't have much to give, you're tired or overwhelmed, I challenge you to light yourself on fire. Don't wait for someone else to do it for you. You have everything you need inside you through the Holy Spirit, and it's time to ignite it. Whether you're feeling overwhelmed, distracted, or unsure of your purpose, I want you to know that you can stir up the power of the Holy Spirit within you. Sometimes, you have to light yourself on fire! I mean that. Sometimes, we wait for inspiration or our emotions to catch up, but God says, "No, you stir up the gift that's already inside you" (2 Timothy 1:6).

The Holy Spirit doesn't need to be recharged like a phone. He's already there, wholly ready, fully powerful. We're the ones who need to remember what we carry. You don't have to wait for perfect circumstances or everything in your life to be right before you can be effective. You have the power of the Holy

Spirit living inside you right now to ignite your spirit. That's what changes everything.

When you stir up the Holy Spirit inside you, it lights a fire in others.

It's not only about you. When you stir up the Holy Spirit inside you, it lights a fire in others, too. People around you will see something different, and it will spark something in them. When you walk into a room full of the Holy Spirit, you don't have to say much—people will feel it.

STAY SENSITIVE TO THE HOLY SPIRIT'S VOICE

Remember, God speaks to each of us differently, and He's always speaking. The Holy Spirit is your guide, whether making a big decision or trying to get through the day. However, you must be tuned in! It's like a radio—you'll miss it if you're not on the right frequency. Sometimes the world gets so loud, but the Holy Spirit whispers to your heart. Stay sensitive to that still, small voice.

I love how the Holy Spirit leads us when Joseph and I make decisions. If we don't have peace to move forward, we won't.

It's the same for you—you can ask God for guidance, and He'll lead you, even in the smallest things. Always trust that inner witness of the Holy Spirit.

Jesus took care of it on the Cross.

The enemy will try to get you to doubt that voice. He'll whisper things such as, "Are you sure that's God? Maybe it's just you." But the more time you spend in God's presence, the more you'll hear His voice. You'll start recognizing when the Holy Spirit is leading you, and that's where the power is. God is not trying to hide His will from you; He's leading you every step of the way.

PRAYING FROM A PLACE OF VICTORY

Here's the thing about prayer—in the New Testament, prayer isn't about begging God to do something for you. We have to stop coming to God as if we are beggars. Jesus already won the victory! When you pray, you're not asking for victory—you're praying from a place of victory. Jesus took care of it on the Cross.

You don't have to plead when you're praying—whether you need healing, help with your finances, peace over your mind, or direction in life. You thank God for what He's done and stand on that truth until you see it happen before you.

We're not in the Old Testament anymore, where Daniel prayed and waited 21 days for an answer because the prince of Persia was resisting (Daniel 10). No, the Holy Spirit is inside you now! You're not waiting on a response from a distant God. The same power that raised Jesus from the dead is living in you, and you have access to it (Romans 8:11). When you pray, you come from a place of power, not weakness.

That's what the first chapter in Ephesians is all about. It's a great reminder to us that everything has already been done. By His stripes, you were healed (Isaiah 53:5). That's past tense. You're already healed.

When you pray, you're not asking God to do something new—you're getting a revelation of what you already have. You're not begging; you're thanking Him, "Thank You, Jesus, that I don't have to live like this anymore. Thank You that I'm already healed. Thank You that I'm already provided for." You're standing in victory, not defeat.

This applies to every situation in your life—whether you're a mom trying to balance life, a business owner facing challenges, or someone dealing with personal struggles. God's power inside you is enough to carry you through. You're not praying from desperation anymore; you're praying from a place of authority and confidence, knowing that God has already provided everything you need.

FINDING YOUR GOSHEN IN GOD'S PRESENCE

As mentioned when we opened this chapter, we live in a world full of chaos. When you turn on the news, it seems as if darkness is everywhere. But we are people of covenant. Just like the Israelites were protected in Goshen while the Egyptians sat in darkness, we have a Goshen, too. I asked the Lord, "Where's our Goshen today?" And He told me, "Your Goshen is in My presence."

Goshen wasn't just a physical location—it was a place where the light of God shone in the middle of darkness. That's what

His presence is for us today. When you stay in the presence of God, there's light in your heart, mind, body, and family. Wherever you go, His light goes with you because His presence goes with you.

Stay in the presence of God—stay in Goshen.

The darkness might feel thick at times. You might feel as if you can't even see your hand in front of your face like there's no way forward. However, just like the Israelites, God has given you a place of light in the middle of it (Exodus 10:23). He's given you His presence, and that's your safe place. That's where you will find peace, clarity, and strength to keep moving forward.

How do you stay in His presence? For me, I'm a worshiper. When I worship, I get lost in His presence. Sometimes I have to ensure I'm not trying to do practical things like laundry simultaneously because I'll get lost in worship, and nothing else gets done!

For you, it might be different. Maybe it's spending time in nature with your Creator or getting lost in His Word. Whatever sparks that fire in you, whatever brings you into His presence—do that. That's your Goshen. That's your safe place in Him.

A GIFT FOR ALL BELIEVERS

Let's talk about speaking in tongues (1 Corinthians 14). I know this topic can be a little controversial, but hear me out—it's one of the most powerful tools you have as a believer. When you pray in the Spirit, you're speaking mysteries to God. You're stirring up things in the Spirit that your natural mind can't comprehend. But here's the beauty of speaking in tongues—it builds you up.

Jude 1:20 (NKJV) says, "But you, beloved, building yourselves up on your most holy faith, praying in the Holy Spirit." When you pray in tongues, you strengthen your faith; the more you do it, the more you start seeing results.

At first when I started praying in tongues, I didn't feel much. But now? Man, sometimes my tongues sound Hispanic, sometimes Asian—it's like the Holy Spirit is speaking through me in different languages! I'm just a vessel, and He's using me. That's the power of the Holy Spirit.

When you pray in tongues, you're releasing the mysteries of God. You're accessing wisdom that you wouldn't get otherwise. It's like building a track record with God. The more you pray in the Spirit, the more answers you get. At first, the answers might be subtle—like a small thought or a solution you hadn't considered—but as you keep going, your confidence grows. Now you're not just hoping for answers but expecting them.

Your prayers are seeds; every seed takes time to grow.

This is where Hebrews 10:35 (NKJV) comes in: "Therefore do not cast away your confidence, which has great reward." The more you get answers, the more confident you become. You start to build history with God; soon, nothing can shake your faith because you know He has your back.

STAND UNTIL THE ANSWER COMES

Maybe you've prayed when it seemed like nothing was happening. You might have even wondered, *"God, where are You in this?"*

Just because you don't see it immediately doesn't mean your answer isn't coming. There's power in standing firm and believing that what you've prayed for will come to pass in God's timing.

The Bible says in Galatians 6:9 (NIV), "Let us not become weary in doing good, for at the proper time we will reap a harvest if we do not give up." Your prayers are seeds, and every seed takes time to grow.

1. Stay steady in your faith.
2. Keep thanking God, even when you don't see the full picture.
3. Believe your harvest is coming.

This is where many people give up—they think a delay means denial. But I'm here to tell you that's not true. God works behind the scenes, even when you don't see it. Don't let go of your faith. Hold on to His promises because He's faithful to bring them to pass.

YOU HAVE AUTHORITY IN CHRIST

When you belong to Jesus, you are not at the mercy of whatever life throws at you. You've been given authority in His name. Luke 10:19 (NIV) says, "I have given you authority to trample on snakes and scorpions and to overcome all the power of the enemy; nothing will harm you."

Too often, we sit back and let the enemy push us around, but God says, "Enough is enough." When the devil comes at you with fear, doubt, or any attack, you stand up and use the authority you've been given. Jesus already won the victory—you have to walk in it.

- Search the Bible for what God has to say about you. (Maybe you see yourself in a prayer the apostle Paul prayed or a psalm David sang.)
- Speak aloud the Word over your life.
- Declare victory over your situation.

The enemy has no power over a child of God who knows their authority.

This authority is for every believer. It's for you. You have the authority to speak peace over your home, pray healing over your body, and declare a breakthrough over your situation. Don't let the enemy make you think otherwise. You're not a victim—you're victorious in Christ.

PROTECT YOUR MIND FROM THE ENEMY'S ATTACKS

The enemy takes pleasure in messing with your mind. He knows that if he can get you thinking the wrong way, he can affect everything in your life. That's why the Bible says to take every thought captive and make it obedient to Christ (2 Corinthians 10:5).

One of the enemy's favorite lies is to get you to believe you're powerless or that God isn't working in your situation. But that's a lie straight from the pit of hell! You have the mind of Christ (1 Corinthians 2:16), which means you don't have to entertain every thought that comes your way.

When those negative thoughts come—thoughts of fear, doubt, or confusion—don't let them linger. Combat them with the truth of God's Word. Speak life over your mind. You are victorious in Christ; no lie from the enemy can change that.

TAG, YOU'RE IT

No matter what's happening in your life, you are not a prisoner of your circumstances. You are not a victim. God's love for you is so great that nothing—not even your past mistakes—can separate you from it. You have the Holy Spirit living inside you, and you are more powerful than you realize (1 Corinthians 3:16).

I know life can feel overwhelming at times. Maybe you feel like the enemy has been chasing you down, but guess what? Now it's your turn. Tag—you're it! The devil better run because it's time for you to do some business with God. You've been chased long enough; it's time to step into your authority.

If you trip, get back up—quick down, quick up. Don't stay down. God's grace is there for you every step of the way. At a conference, I was walking down this grand staircase in heels and tripped. But in a split second, I was back up, smiling, *I'm fine!*

That's how it is with the Holy Spirit—quick down, quick up. When you're praying in the Spirit, you get back up faster, and what used to take a long time to recover now comes quickly. God's grace works in you, and He has more blessings for you than you can imagine.

THE FIGHT AHEAD IS ALREADY WON

As we close this chapter and this book, I want to leave you with one final truth: *the fight ahead is already won.* Whatever battles you face, whatever challenges come your way, you are not alone, and you are not powerless. The same God who walked with me through every trial, heartbreak, and victory is the same God walking with you now.

You've read my story, but now it's time for you to live yours. What will you do with what you've learned? Will you stand up in the power of the Holy Spirit, knowing that you're already victorious? Will you press into His presence, even when life feels overwhelming? I pray that you will because there's a world out there waiting for what God has placed inside you.

You don't have to be perfect or have all the answers. You have to say yes to God and take the next step in faith. The Holy Spirit will guide, empower, and give you everything you need. You've been born with a purpose; you have assignments.

So go—walk in the authority that's already yours. Speak God's promises over your life. Stay in His presence. Let His fire burn brightly in you and light the way for others. The enemy may try to come against you, but he doesn't stand a chance against a child of God who knows their worth, authority, and victory in Christ.

As you go, remember: God's got you. He always has and always will. Your journey to wholeness is a testament to His faithfulness, and your story is far from over.

Let's seal the time we've had together in prayer.

> *Father, thank You for every person who has walked through this journey with me. I pray that You would ignite a fire in their hearts that cannot be quenched. Remind them of who they are in You and the power they carry through the Holy Spirit. Lord, let Your presence be their safe place, their Goshen in the midst of any storm. I speak life, peace, and victory over every reader. May they boldly and confidently walk in the fullness of Your promises, knowing that You've already won every battle they will ever face. We give You all the glory, Lord, and we thank You for what's to come. In Jesus' name, amen.*

Now go and walk in victory. God is with you!

ABOUT HEATHER Z

A powerful voice for freedom, healing, and hope in God, Heather Z's greatest passion is seeing people set free from the restraints that keep them from stepping into the fullness of their God-given purpose. Whether through prayer, teaching, or simply walking alongside others in their faith journey, Heather is convinced that no burden is too heavy and no life is too broken for God to restore.

As a young teen, Heather survived a devastating accident that caused a broken neck. What should have ended her story became the beginning of a miraculous journey. She left her body and traveled to an in-between place. God miraculously healed her, igniting a faith that has touched thousands of others.

For almost 20 years, Heather and her husband, Joseph Z, have served in churches, conferences, and ministries worldwide, helping people experience God's presence and power in deeply personal ways. Known for her boldness in prayer and her unwavering belief in wholeness, Heather has witnessed lives changed through physical healing, emotional breakthroughs, and lifting of spiritual burdens.

Heather's heart goes beyond the miraculous—it's about connection. She has an extraordinary ability to see people where they are, identify their struggles, and lovingly guide them toward freedom through God's Word. Her teachings are as practical as they are powerful, equipping others to step out of fear and into the abundant life God has for them.

Heather believes that the same God who healed, restored, and made her whole can move in your life, too. Whether you're battling doubt, seeking healing, or feeling stuck, Heather wants you to know God and realize He is ready to meet you where you are, break every chain, and lead you into the life you were made for.

ZMINISTRIES
BUILDING LIVES BY THE VOICE OF GOD

Joseph and Heather have ministered together for over 20 years; with a passion to see others be all they are called to be. For many years, Joseph & Heather have had the heart to offer life-changing materials and teaching at no cost to the body of Christ. Today, they have made that a reality by offering various media resources and biblical training free of charge. Joseph and Heather currently reside in Colorado Springs, CO with their two children, Alison and Daniel.

Learn more at
www.josephz.com